CW00556592

MYTHS OF GODS AND GODDESSES

IN BRITAIN AND IRELAND

MYTHS OF GODS AND GODDESSES

IN BRITAIN AND IRELAND

SHARON
JACKSTIES

For Hugh and Eric,
with love and gratitude for more journeys
than steps and more stories than words

First published 2022

The History Press
97 St George's Place, Cheltenham,
Gloucestershire, GL50 3QB
www.thehistorypress.co.uk

British Library Cataloguing in Publication Data.
A catalogue record for this book is available from the British Library.

ISBN 978 0 7509 9563 4

Typesetting and origination by The History Press
Printed and bound in Great Britain by TJ Books Limited, Padstow, Cornwall.

MIX
Paper from
responsible sources
FSC® C013056
www.fsc.org

Trees for Life

CONTENTS

INTRODUCTION

During my career as an oral storyteller, I have been lucky enough to be introduced to our great mythic heritage by the best of traditional tellers, who have made it their lives' work to craft mythological tales into forms that can survive a fragmented oral tradition. The disruption of oral storytelling has been brought about by technology, the Industrial Revolution and the cultural suppression that accompanies colonialism. This last, however, can also be a spur for people to preserve and celebrate their threatened heritage.

Unlike the rest of the world, these islands have mostly lost that canon of traditional narratives that storytellers and ethnologists call 'creation myths' – those stories that tell us how the very fabric of our land, and even the universe, were created. I am, therefore, deeply grateful, during one of the Covid-19 pandemic lockdowns, to have been transported, if not in place, but in time, listening online to some storytellers in the Scottish International Storytelling Festival telling what must be the most intact British creation story from this earliest genre of myth.

The Cailleach, Old Woman, remembered also in Ireland, is with us still in our seasons and landscapes. She too can speak to us amidst our increasing concerns for our environment and the natural world. Enduring as the Scottish granite she created, she has survived the transition from the veneration of the Mother Earth goddess to that of the patriarchal Sky Gods, precursors to a single male patriarchy.

Recent astronomical discoveries have shown that this change in focus occurred during a period of prolonged meteoric activity, when our night skies were literally blazing with light, as waves of comets shot across our heavens like divine spears – such potent symbols and power objects in our later mythology of gods and superheroes. Archaeology, too, reflects this fundamental change, seen in our stone circles and megalithic monuments. This physical evidence from a uniquely Irish and British heritage is testament to our ancestor's religious relationship with the celestial bodies, stone built from the element of Mother Earth herself, and connecting the old Goddess with the increasing worship of the Sky Gods. Ranging across these sacred sites strides a pantheon of divinities: goddesses and gods to be joined with and superseded by pantheons from other parts of Europe and beyond. How long these sacred, vertical stone bridges between earth and sky, these terrestrial maps of the movements of the heavens were venerated, is impossible to say. Some would protest that they have never ceased to be held sacred. Others were introduced later, such as the Roman Mithraeums and shrines dedicated to a divinity that originated at least as far east as ancient Persia. Mithras, too was worshipped in Britain, and readers should not be surprised to come across a creation myth from such a distant visitor.

A storyteller's journey, therefore, is one that travels through time as well as place, and perhaps an early understanding of this came half a lifetime ago, when I was an emerging storyteller, I regularly visited a remote district in an Irish-speaking part of Ulster. In those days the bank consisted of a van that would set up its services in someone's living room for half a day every week, and apart from an occasional bus, any connection with the wider world was through the post office. There I was buying stamps when I noticed that their illustration could only be from the story that, unlike many from the oral tradition, is so well known that it has a title. I was so excited to notice this official celebration of traditional literature that my clipped BBC English rang out: 'But these must be the Children of Lir!'

At that, the screen rattled down and the post master burst out of his kiosk. Business was over and joy was about to begin. There he stood, small, fat and bald, yet transformed by some enchanting glamour as he launched into that story, in his own language. Eyes half closed, his pudgy hands gesturing magnificently, he held forth in this poetic narrative medium. The queue stood there equally spellbound whether we could understand Irish or not. When he finished, he was met with a profound silence, more eloquent and complimentary than any applause. Mythology, as it was meant to be, in its oral and aural forms was, for a while, alive and well. I had been part of its sharing and, during those precious timeless moments, there had been little difference between myself and those listeners from distant millennia.

My move from London to Somerset inspired a less eclectic approach to my international repertoire, and enabled me to focus more deeply on regional material. This process led to my becoming an author of collections of local traditional tales. During a storytelling project called TheMaking of Wessex, I explored the story legacies left to us by the various cultures that had traded with, settled in, conquered or converted Britain and

Ireland. From the Bronze Age to the Early Christian era, it was clear that Britain and Ireland are repositories for this overlay of mythologies, and this comparatively small geographical area is the custodian of the major traditional stories, folk tales and myths from the whole of Europe.

Readers may be surprised to discover stories of characters that we do not think of today as being divine. Let me plead for their reinstatement, if only in our imaginations, after millennia of being demoted by a 'jealous God' whose priests were eager to denigrate any perceived competition from other powerful beings. So it was, for example, that a Brythonic Celtic god of light, Gwyn ap Neath, became denigrated to the 'King of the Fairies' in his Underworld, where he was humiliated and defeated by a Christian saint. Others of his ilk eventually became the folklore characters of superstition – witches, imps, goblins and the like – their magical powers slandered as being in service to the Devil or dismissed as fairy tales only fit for children. Rare examples exist, however, of various powerful entities – mortal rulers, gods and fairy royalty – all co-operating from within their respective sovereign realms, such as in the tale I have entitled 'Dream Lover'.

Other divinities underwent a kinder transformation, becoming our first superheroes, often characters with at least one divine parent, who although mortal, are remembered for their superhuman exploits, accomplished through more than mortal powers. It is said of Finn mac Cumhaill, one of the greatest of these heroes, that if a day goes by without one of his stories being told, that will be the day when our world will end. He has thereby reclaimed the immortality to which he is entitled. He and his mythological kindred continue to have their lives rekindled in our collective memory, through story.

We tend to think of the Irish/Scottish and Brythonic Celts, Iron Age peoples, as providers of our oldest stories. However, as with all peoples, the tales are older than those who told them and these Bronze Age myths conceal even earlier antecedents. Set in a pantheistic age, they contain features from an earlier belief system, that of Animism. The shape-shifting so prevalent among the protagonists in this book recall the transformations experienced by the most powerful among ancient peoples – their shamans. The focus on travelling between different worlds – underworlds, other worlds, those of fairies, monsters or giants – also recall the out-of-body experiences that enabled shamans to travel between this world and others. Another striking example of animistic belief survives in the Norse myth, here entitled 'Baldur Betrayed', in which every object becomes animate, whether tree or rock or metal. In this collection, therefore, we have Bronze Age stories told by Iron Age people in which also appear the animistic beliefs of our earliest Stone Age ancestors.

Perhaps readers will also be surprised to discover stories of Roman and Norse origin in this volume. I have tried to restrict myself to including those that are specifically depicted in the archaeology to be found throughout Britain. It is impossible to imagine people living in Roman villas (in what are now Somerset and Dorset, for example), in which, at vast expense for their time, mosaics displayed the myths of Dido and Aeneas or Bellerophon, without their inhabitants being acquainted with their stories. Dinner guests would have admired and referred to them, mothers and slaves would have told these illustrated tales to children, and tutors would have included them as part of a formal curriculum. Fascinating too, are the depictions of events from Norse mythology, sharing space on Christian crosses and in church architecture – a narrative overlay that demonstrates how cultures absorb and transform each other.

I was discussing with a colleague how 'foreign' cultures become absorbed, and how, through longevity, they become accepted as 'native'. I was using Dorset's mosaic of Bellerophon slaying the monstrous Chimaera as an example, an art work that I had known of, but had never examined, and therefore was unaware of its other significance. Neither did I know that this colleague, on a college placement, was one of the first archaeologists on the site where that mosaic was discovered. Suddenly, as she was digging, she saw a face staring up at her. This part of the mosaic proved to be the earliest-known portrait of Jesus and she was the first to see it for many hundreds of years. There it lay, docile neighbour with Bellerophon and his monstrous Chimaera, a hero from a polytheistic religion whose iconography so resembled that which was to become a renowned Christian symbol – that of St George and the Dragon. Roman Christianity had reached Britain.

Little remains of our oldest civilisations apart from stone monuments, archaeological artefacts and, of course, a body of oral literature preserved by storytellers and, centuries later, in written form. Irish/Scottish and Brythonic Celts brought us their stories, and 'brought' is a careful word as their mythology speaks of waves of discovery and conquests of Ireland, and Britain by an incoming people. Their tales of the divine conquest of a brutish race, the Formorians, have close parallels with the classical Graeco–Roman myths of gods and goddesses defeating Titans, and the Norse examples of gods and goddesses warring with giants. Readers will notice many other similarities among these different mythologies. This phenomenon led me to consider how many Celts came westwards through a region that we now call Greece, and how the Vikings' trading routes travelled through these regions and to Ireland for many hundreds of years. Small wonder that motifs and narratives were shared, repeated and survived any particular cultural cachets to an extraordinary degree of detail within storylines, whispering of a pan-European mythology that came to rest at its most westerly border.

A Divine Conference in British Weather

There could not have been a single Roman soldier who relished a posting to Britain and its foul climate. There, treacherous tribes refused to lie down and surrender, the most fearsome warriors were often women, and the mud was impossible to march through. Any part of Britain would have been bad enough, but the very worst that could happen was to be sent to Hadrian's Wall. That was the northern limit of the mighty Roman Empire, but not even the Romans had managed to conquer the unruly Picts who lived beyond it. The best that could be done was to prevent their raiding parties from penetrating any further south. How the wind howled and the rain lashed on top of the wall as the sentries looked out over unconquered territory.

On this particular summer's day a sentry was trying to see through the gloom that this especially vicious storm had brought, along with the torrential rain, thunder, lightning and hailstones the size of hen's eggs. His bare knees were as blue as the woad that adorned his enemies and if he had seen any, he knew that he would have been too cold to do anything about it. Misery permeated every cell of his body and he was shivering too violently even to accurately wipe his streaming nose with his sodden tunic.

History does not reveal the name of this unhappy soldier, so from a sense of irony I will call him 'Felix' or 'Lucky', just as nicknames are sometimes bestowed on those who display an opposite characteristic. Felix was wondering whether his name, which also means 'cat' in Latin, had somehow been responsible for getting him this posting. This was because the local unconquerable tribe's totem animal was the wildcat, who, just like the people it represented, was elusive, cunning and disproportionately vicious for its size. Suddenly his shivering form was lit up by an almost direct hit as lightning struck the wall, making him tremble even more.

But the Gods had seen him! All the gods of thunder and storm who ruled over that land had not only noticed, but even more surprisingly had taken pity on that miserable specimen of mortality. Jupiter from the Roman pantheon, Thor from the Norse and Manannàn mac Lir from the Celtic, were in a huddle wondering what they could do for him, as each believed themselves responsible for the storm that had brought Felix such discomfort.

As they were discussing this between them, more divinities arrived to add their opinions. Wasn't the mortal a soldier? Shouldn't the gods or goddesses of war be consulted? Representing those three pantheons again, Mars, Odin and the Morrigan joined the divine throng on the storm clouds. The discussion became more animated, gestures became more expansive, clouds were pummelled like cushions and hailstones flew like feathers. Surely what the man needed was comfort, but what kind of comfort? At this any divinities of love who may have been listening in, such as Aphrodite, Freya or Aengus, melted into the distance.

What was needed was something sustaining to warm him, preferably from the inside out. All the gods and goddesses agreed about that.

The clouds got even thicker to accommodate another wave of divinities who had arrived to suggest their remedies. All of these consisted of alcoholic beverages, and Ceres, The Dagda, Aegir and Gobniu attempted to convince the divine assembly of the uniquely reviving properties of their particular brew and of their right thereby in assisting the mortal.

Was not Ceres Goddess of Crops and Harvests? Did not her grain grow over the largest area of the Earth? How would any beer be made without her gift of fertility? Strong arguments indeed. However, Dagda the Good, father of the Irish Gods, spoke up and explained that he had a magical cauldron that was always full of beer, a source that would never run out. Surely he should be the one to share this bounty? Another strong argument. Then Aegir explained why he should be the one to offer the remedy, as he was the host of all the Norse gods and goddesses who came to sample his beer in his drinking hall under the sea. There they were served in an atmosphere of conviviality. No bad behaviour was tolerated – and as with many publicans centuries later, any misbehaviour resulted in the perpetrator being barred – and in his case any overindulgence was explained by the rocking and tilting of the sea. All strong arguments.

Never had so many deities from so many religions attempted to do so much for so few. Jupiter could see that they were in a situation of overkill, and feared any competition escalating into conflict between pantheons that existed so peaceably together.

He suggested that as the mortal was a Roman, newly sent from the capital of the Roman Empire, he, as a Roman god should be responsible for any outcome. He also decided to supply the soldier with a new kind of remedy, rather than allowing any competitiveness about beer to flourish. Before anyone else could think of a counter-argument, there was another flash of lightning that burned a small crater near to the hapless mortal. Peering into it when the smoke had dissipated, he noticed to his surprise that something vividly green lay there.

Curiosity overcame fear and he retrieved a strange-looking plant, complete with roots, a tiny stem and twisting tendrils with bright green leaves. At first he had no idea what to do with it, but knew that it had to be treasured as it was clearly a gift from Jupiter. Guessing that he should perhaps nurture it like some kind of delicate plant, he dug up some soil but then didn't know what to put it in. Looking around, he saw a bird's skull and gently tucked shoot and earth into that. It was astonishing how quickly this divine gift grew. Within a few days the roots were pushing through the eye sockets and the length of the stem had made the tiny vessel topple over. It would need to be transplanted into something bigger that also allowed for this rapid growth rate. On patrol, he had come across a bear's skull. This curiosity was ideal for a while, but the vigorous plant soon outgrew that too. Another container was found – an ass' skull. By now the grape vine was bearing grapes and wine had been made from them. From that day to this, when we drink a little we are inclined to sing, merry as birds. If we drink rather more, we gain the courage of a bear, but if we drink more than that, we sound and act like an ass.

1

CHILDREN BORN OF POWER, CHILDREN BORN OF MAGIC

… There are two ways to live your life. One is as though nothing is a miracle. The other is as though everything is a miracle …

Albert Einstein

ARIANRHOD, GODDESS OF THE SILVER WHEEL

Arianrhod was born into a family of the greatest magicians that Wales has ever known. It was said that only the ancient gods had powers such as theirs – small wonder then, as Arianrhod was the daughter of the great Mother Goddess herself. However, when their stories were finally written down, hundreds of years later in the time of the new religion, these beings of divine power were reduced to mere kings and queens, lords and ladies among the mortals of the land.

In the days when Wales had several rulers, none could equal Math or his family in the practice of magic. His nephew Gwydion's art lay in the magic of illusion and transformation – the seeming and the un-seeming that could make one thing appear to be another. These illusions were mostly short-lived but quickened to the length of their purpose. He would use any form of trickery to his own ends, and these were such that it was often the only way he could get what he wanted.

Math's niece, Arianrhod, was moved by an older magic, one that was shaped by the elements themselves, the powers that brought life to land or water or air. It was these forces that moved through Arianrhod as she sought to blend their power with hers, rather than keeping company with those who thronged her uncle's court. Not for her the soft cushions, the sweet musicians, the whispered gossip of court scandal. She took her ease on rough granite, her music was the roaring of waves and her conversation the whispering of the wind. For Arianrhod lived far away in a deserted spot, her home a craggy castle at the tip of the land, surrounded on three sides by wild waters, overarched by the wide sky.

Mighty though Lord Math was, he had one strange peculiarity: unless he was at war, he could not put his feet upon the ground while at rest. To do so would be to risk his life. That is why his feet always needed to be placed in the lap of a maiden, whose purity was the only thing that could protect him from this strange weakness. Goewin, a pure and gentle young woman, was always on hand for this purpose. In times of peace she followed him everywhere in case she was needed.

'Happy is the man even if it is only Goewin's shadow that falls upon him,' Lord Math would say about her. There was none as lovely in the whole land and Math protected her as she protected him.

Arianrhod and Gwydion had another brother, but whatever magical powers Gilfaethwy may have had, they were no help to him in his affliction. He had fallen in love with Goewin and was pining away. At last Gwydion took pity on his brother and decided by use of trickery to embroil his uncle in a war, so that Goewin would be left unprotected. That is how Gilfaethwy was left free to violate the object of his passion – and Math returned to discover the full extent of the treachery. The brothers would have to be punished and another maiden found before his own weakness could take hold, now that he was no longer at war. Eager to re-ingratiate himself with his uncle, Gwydion suggested his sister Arianrhod, and a messenger was hurriedly dispatched to her distant castle.

There she sat spinning a thread made from streams of moonlight brought to her on the incoming tide, twisting them together with filaments she had teased from veils of starlight. As she wove she sang, and her song turned her silver wheel as it hung low on the horizon – the silver wheel that others in a later tongue would call the Corona Borealis. For hers was the magic of the night sky, the cool touch of moon and stars, the places beneath rock and earth that never knew the light. The threads she spun on her wheel were a guide for those who passed from this world into another, dreaming their way onward, then following them once more to find their way back again. Her silver wheel turned to a song she had heard from the greatest bard that the land of Britain had ever known: Taliesin's words brightened moonlight, shimmered starlight as she sang, 'I know all the names of the stars from north to south, I have been in the galaxy at the throne of the One who allocates generously, three times have I been in Arianrhod's prison …'

As her silver wheel sank closer to the sea she thought of all those who had sat on her perfect throne in her wheeling castle – those whose journeys she had guided between the worlds – who always left with their gleaming, silken thread of destiny in their grasp. Some knew her turning castle to be the sky itself, the stars its windows. Some believed that as they sat upon Arianrhod's peerless seat, that the sky wheeled around that place of vision, and that each star was a window into another world. But tonight she was spinning a different thread, a life-giving cord that was also a secret, twisted with the very elements from which this secret life had sprung, a cord that she would keep closer to her than anyone could know.

The court messenger arrived as Arianrhod's silver wheel was about to disappear into the sea. It was an unchancy moment to be interrupted, the wheel's cycle was not complete, and she knew that no good would come of it.

Math's court fell silent as Arianrhod paused at the threshold – too hastily called away from her task, she blinked in that place where people turned night into day. Fires burned, lights blazed, jewels glittered. Her dazzled eyes sought her uncle to greet him first, as was fitting. Then she could see how pale he looked, how weak he had become without his lap maiden. Lady Goewin sprang up. Now full of hope, she embraced Arianrhod, the woman who had been her friend and who was now her kinswoman, for Math had married her as soon as he had heard how she had been used by his nephews. He would not suffer her to be dishonoured and raised her up by making her the first lady in the land. Dishonour would fall on the perpetrators of the crime, not their victim. Punishment and ridicule were to follow as certain as day follows night, but there was a more urgent matter at hand.

'Have you ever lain with a man?' Math demanded of his niece.

'Never, my Lord, how would I when there is none to match me?

Math looked at his niece and could tell that there was, nevertheless, something that she was not telling him. He took up his magic wand and slowly, before the court, bent it in his hands. Everyone knew that Truth itself would straighten it, but that in the presence of falsehood it would remain bent. He placed it on the floor before her, and everyone watched her take the test. As she stepped over the wand, Arianrhod parted her legs to do so, and from her body slipped a fully formed boy child. His cry rang out in that place of sudden light, and his mother sprang for the door. Fast as an autumn wind she moved, but she was not quick enough to keep the other life that should also have stayed inside her. As she took another step, something else slipped from between her legs, something that as yet had no shape. People hardly noticed it, all eyes were upon that storming fury, Arianrhod, as she rushed from the room. But Gwydion, with his magician's eye, could see his nephew's shape to come. Quick as a snake he darted down and scooped up the formless thing, in the same movement wrapping it in his silken cloak. He then placed it in a chest in his private chamber.

Everyone stared at the little boy, sturdy, strong, already standing as no mortal newborn could do. From him came the smell of the sea, while his strong chest heaved with the swell of the waves. Math's magician's eye could see that this little one indeed did not have a human father. He was a child of the Sea God himself – his niece had become pregnant when she had been swimming in the sea. To honour the boy's father, Math had the boy baptised 'Dylan', which is one of the names of the God of the Sea. But it wasn't enough to keep the child in that place. The salt water of the sea had a stronger pull than the sweet water of baptism. On legs so powerful that no one could keep up with him, faster than any flood tide, the boy ran to the shore. Those who had followed saw him dive and frolic in the water, riding every wave.

It was Gwydion who raised the other child, but until he came to manhood, his mother sought to shield him from the corrupting ways of the court. She tried to protect him from the trickery, the seeming/un-seeming deception, of his uncle's kind of magic. She wanted him to know his maternal heritage, the raw elemental power of the old magic. She wanted him to know more than the new religion that showed no respect for the old. Three times she tried to utter a different fate for him, one that should never have been his, but one that would keep him from being swallowed up in her brother's world. Each time she was thwarted by Gwydion's skill. It was only when the young man was close to dying that he felt his true father's power stir inside him. The element of air that had given him life as Arianrhod's throne wheeled about the sky, now gave him the power to save himself, when, mortally wounded, he escaped his attacker in the form of a bird.

So it was that Arianrhod gave birth to her twins before her time, before her silver wheel could finish spinning the silver thread of their destiny twined with their father's elements of water and air. Those who did not have the knowledge saw her leave Math's court a shamed woman. But there were those who knew that she left in anger, never to return, and that any shame should perhaps be theirs.

DEER CHILD, PIG CHILD, WOLF CHILD

Math the magician, lord of Gwynedd, waited for the return of his fugitive nephews. They well knew they were to be punished for the terrible crimes they had committed. His nephew,

Gwydion, as great a magician as himself, had contrived a trap for his uncle that had resulted in Math's most beloved maiden being left unprotected so that she could be raped. Although everyone in the court knew what was happening – her servants had been hustled out of her chamber and everyone could hear her screams – they were all too frightened of Gwydion to interfere, so his brother Gilfaethwy made the most of the opportunity to violate the young woman. Gwydion had arranged all this because he believed that his brother would otherwise die from unrequited passion, despite knowing that this would threaten his uncle's life as Math had to rest his feet in the lap of a virgin when not engaged in war. This decoy of ill-cast magic and trickery had also resulted in a gift from the God of the Other World being stolen, the violation of the sacred law of hospitality, a war between the north and the south of the country, the loss of many innocent lives and the death of the country's greatest hero. Enough, surely, to merit punishment.

At last Math gave an order that no one in all the land was to give his nephews hospitality. If they were starved out they would have to return home sooner or later. The fugitives held out for as long as they could but eventually returned to their uncle's court. Were they shamefaced? Did they try to brazen it out? Before everyone, they greeted Lord Math and asked him what was his will.

'It was not my will to lose all those brave men and their weapons. It was not my will that you shamed me by raping a maiden in my own bed, dearly beloved as she was, and a protector of my own life. It was not my will that you caused the death of Pryderi, greatest of heroes. But if you have come to submit to my will, it is for you to receive your punishment.'

Math struck Gilfaethwy with his wand, turning the man into a hind. Seeing this, Gwydion tried to escape, but his uncle was too quick for him and struck him also, turning him into a stag. Now that they were male and female in animal form, they were bound to mate like animals. But being also human, they were to suffer the humiliation of incest, of bestiality, of being forced into another gender.

'Since you have already conspired unlawfully together, let you mate together, it will be no worse than what you have already done. Live like animals in these animal shapes and return to me in a year's time.'

A year passed and a day came when all the dogs in the court began to bay and howl. Math was told that a stag, a hind and a fawn had appeared. He rose to see for himself and instantly raised his wand.

'He who has been a hind for this past year will be a boar for the next. He who has been a stag for the past year will be a sow for the next. Now go and live out your animal natures for that time.'

The wand touched all the animals, but the fawn was now changed into a boy, his first moment of being in human shape.

'You I will baptise and your name will mean "little stag" and I will find you other parents, for you will be fostered in my realm.'

Another year passed, again the clamour of overexcited dogs was heard. This time a boar, a sow and a piglet, large for his age, stood outside. Again Math flourished his wand.

'You who were a boar will be a she-wolf and you who were a sow will be a wolf. For a year you will live as the wild wolves live.' But the piglet was now a tall lad, his first moment in human form.

'You I will baptise and your name will mean "tall standing piglet" and I will find you other parents, for you will be fostered in my realm.'

At the end of the third year, there was another great disturbance from the dogs and outside were a wolf, a she-wolf and a wolf cub. This time the touch of Math's wand left them all in human form. He said to the boy, 'You I will baptise and your name will mean "little wolf" and I will find you other parents, for you will be fostered in my realm.'

Then Lord Math looked at the men, his nephews who had wronged his beloved maiden and all the land of Wales, 'Behold your three sons. The three sons of wicked Gilfaethwy, it is they who are true champions, Little Stag, Tall Standing Piglet and Little Wolf.'

Lord Math did not visit the wickedness of their parents onto those children. They were respected and cared for and it is said that one could run as fast as the deer, that another could smell out anything both good or bad and that the last was as tireless as a wolf.

CHILD PROPHET

When Roman rule ended, Britain became an arena of strife between kings, chiefs and rulers of every kind. For decade after decade, war flourished between petty kingdoms, and the ones who profited most were Britain's invaders. The golden age when this land had been known as the Island of the Mighty was long gone, and her goddesses and heroes were remembered in stories around the watch fires as depleted forces waited for more raiders from the sea. These raiders had soon become warring settlers and treaties were made and broken with the Britons, strengthening enmities and creating new conflicts. On occasion it became expedient to side with the invaders for one's own protection or to hold onto increasingly precarious power. One such warlord was Vortigern, hated mostly for making treaties with the Saxons rather than defeating them – a strategy of appeasement that failed and contributed to the annexing of a large part of the country by the invaders.

Unpopularity, however, rarely diminishes vanity, and Vortigern sought to aggrandise himself by building an immense tower. Some said it was to be a watchtower so that he could see his enemies from afar, some said it was so that his soothsayers could predict the future by observing the portents in the heavens. But however strongly it was built, and however many times it was rebuilt, it always tumbled down. At last Vortigern consulted his soothsayers and was told that the only way to be successful was to sacrifice a boy who had been conceived without a father and pour his blood on the stones.

They set off to find such a one, searching throughout the land without success. At last, when they had almost given up, they were idly watching a group of raggedy boys playing ball. Suddenly the usual laddish taunts took on another tone – one that caught Vortigern's attention and made him listen rather than merely hear. They were mocking one of their number for never having had a father – but surely there were so many children brought up without fathers in these lawless times. This could be such a common insult that it was hardly worth using it as a means of singling someone out for cruel attention. Perhaps, instead, there was something captivating in their victim's demeanour: his refusal to give ground, his unflinching cold gaze and the contemptuous curl of his lip. Perhaps, at last, this was the one they had been looking for. Strange too, that he did not move when Vortigern called him over. Stranger still that Vortigern found himself going over to the boy despite being disobeyed.

The two looked each other over, one with a cunning and speculative gleam in his eye, the other with cold contempt.

'They say you have no father.'

The boy said nothing and did not avert his gaze. But now Vortigern noticed that the child was no longer looking at him, even though he had not moved his eyes. It felt as though the boy was looking through and past him at something that made that contemptuous mouth set in triumph.

'Tell me about your father.'

'Indeed there is a rare story to be told about him, and my mother, a virgin nun locked up in a convent. They say that an evil spirit came to her in the night, intent on fathering a demon child whose life's work would be to pit itself, with superhuman powers, against all that was good. For this plan to come about, Evil would have to corrupt the purest, the peerless of the land. Such a woman was my mother. Even now, such a woman *is* my mother. They say that this evil being took on the form of one who couples with those who are asleep – an incubus, they said. But after the deed was done, when my mother awoke, she knew that what she remembered was something more than a nightmare. She ran to the mother superior and demanded that a priest was summoned even though it was the middle of the night. Her insistence was so different from her customary meekness that the abbess had the wit to realise that something untoward had happened. The priest was sent for and performed a rite of exorcism. I survived, but the evil did not. My one legacy from my father – if you would call him that, for he was never a man – is that I have a strange way of looking at things and a stranger way of seeing and of being seen – all beyond your imagining. Why, for instance, would I come at your call when I know that you intend to murder me?'

Vortigern and his company felt rooted to the spot as the youth brought his gaze to play upon them, washing them in cold fire. His speech flicked around them like a silken whip, corralling them together. Each word was a silken thread that wove with the next until all were caught in the net of the boy's knowing.

'Your court soothsayers, magicians, call them what you will, your "false prophets" have indeed played you false. No sacrifice of me or daubing of my blood will prevent your tower from falling. Ask them what is beneath the foundations of your tottering tower.'

Vortigern's retinue could not answer because they did not know.

'Beneath your tower lies a great pool of water. I will come with you now to the place, so that I may watch as you order the workmen to dig up the foundations. I want to see the look on your false prophets' faces when they see that I am right.'

All came to pass as the youth had said. Then he asked, 'And now can your false prophets tell you what lies beneath that water?'

Knowing that they couldn't, he went on to say, 'If you drain the pool, you will find two great stones. Inside the stones, two dragons sleep, one red, one white. As night falls they awaken and rise, already fighting, into the sky. All night they fight and their roiling combat makes the tower tremble and fall. The white dragon is the Saxon hordes that seek to swallow this island. The red dragon is the Britons who cling to what is theirs. Time and time again, the white dragon beats the red, but there will come a time when the tide of strife turns, and the red dragon will drive the white from the Island of the Mighty, from this land of Britain. The people will unite under the sign of the Boar of Cornwall to follow the way of the Red Dragon. But that will be in my time, and spell the ending of your time. And from that time I will be known, and remembered for all time, as Merlin.

FOSTER MOTHER, VIRGIN MOTHER, MARRIED MOTHER

Deichtine, the chief's daughter, was also her father's charioteer. There wasn't a woman to match her in courage, endurance and beauty. One day when the chief's retinue were visiting the vast plain of Ulster, they saw that a strange flock of birds had alighted and were proceeding to devour every living plant, wild or cultivated. Before long, the plain had been turned into a desert and everyone feared that the flock would move on until the whole land was devastated. They decided to chase the flock away. This would give them sport too, as they delighted in the hunting of birds, and the most favoured of the women would wear wings and feathers in their hair. Off they all went, with Deichtine driving her father in his chariot. On they travelled beneath a cloud of many hundreds of these beautiful white creatures, dazzled by the light from the silver chains that joined each pair, enchanted by their magical singing.

As night fell, three of the birds parted from the others and flew off towards the sacred place we in England now call New Grange. This was one of the homes of the Gods, the gateway between our world and theirs. It was here that every midwinter, Lugh, God of Light and Sun, would renew his promise to always return to this world in its darkest hour. There could be no more auspicious an omen and even Bricriu, with his troublemaking nature and his malicious tongue, was pleased to follow. That night it was as though all the bird's feathers had fallen from the sky, so soft and white a snow it was that now covered the ground. It was impossible for chariots to move any further, and the chief ordered that a group went ahead to look for shelter. Ever eager for comfort, Bricriu was among them and soon they came upon a house that was obviously newly built. Although they were welcomed by the couple who owned it, Bricriu complained that it was too small and didn't have a storehouse full of food and dry clothes to offer them. Nevertheless, the chief decided to accept whatever hospitality had been offered whether great or small, and the company arrived at the house. It was as though accepting that humble invitation had made the gift of plenty appear, for suddenly there appeared a brimming store house and soon all were well feasted and merry with good wine. In the warmth of welcome and good cheer, the host approached Deichtine to say that his wife had gone into labour in the storehouse. Immediately, Deichtine sprang to help and before long a baby boy was born. At that same moment, one of the chieftain's mares gave birth to twin foals and these were given as a gift to the newborn of the house, who Deichtine was now nursing as though he were her own.

When the next day dawned, all the guests found themselves some distance away from New Grange and all that they expected to see of their new surroundings had disappeared – now there was no house nor any birds, only the baby boy with his two foals. So the company returned to the plain and Deichtine loved and cared for her baby foster son, who grew into boyhood but then died. She wept for many days and after shedding so many tears grew so thirsty that she asked for a copper pot to drink from. However, every time she put the rim to her lips, something tiny and luminous wriggled through the water and tried to jump into her mouth. But whenever she looked into the pot, she could see nothing and being so consumed by thirst she drank the contents anyway. That night she dreamed that a man named Lugh spoke to her, saying that it was he who had brought her to New Grange and that she was now pregnant by him and that their son was to be called Setanta. Some say that the name means 'Wisdom of the Ways'.

Soon it became obvious that the chief's daughter was expecting a child, and the court was concerned at not knowing who the father was. A rumour started that she had been made pregnant by her own father when he was drunk, and it would have been no surprise if it had been discovered that Bricriu had started it. But what could Deichtine say? That she had been made pregnant by the contents of a copper pot with a drink that had something small and bright in it that tried to wriggle and jump into her mouth? That she had heard a man's voice in a dream calling himself Lugh but that the man himself could not be seen? She decided to remain silent rather than add folly to scandal, and allowed her father to quickly find a husband for her before the baby was born so that it would be acknowledged as his. However, before her wedding night to Sualtaim, wanting to appear as a bride and not a mother, she rolled over and over onto her full belly until she thought she had crushed the child that was inside her. That same night when she lay with her husband, she conceived, and when the boy was born he was named Setanta.

Others say that the name means 'Mythical son of Sualtaim'. Some say that Deichtine had never been pregnant twice and had not managed to destroy her baby after all; he was only waiting to be born at a time when he would be accepted as being their husband's natural son. Some said that this magical child had two fathers, one of this world and one of the Other World, one mortal and one divine, and that the different meanings of his name were both true.

CHILD CHAMPION

Setanta was barely six years old when he wanted to join the older boys at their games, all of which were martial and involved every kind of fighting and weaponry. At first his mother refused to let him go but soon realised that he was so determined that she could not prevent him. Off he went on the long journey to where the boys were being trained to become the best soldiers in the land. To amuse himself and make the journey shorter, he would fling his toy javelin ahead of him and catch it before it could even reach the ground, leaving only the half print of running footsteps in the dust and those further apart than any springing deer.

Setanta had not met any of the boys before and did not know their customs. He did not know that he should not set foot upon their training ground without first asking for their protection. In doing so he aroused their anger, even more so because they could tell that he was one of their tribe and should have known better. They warned him to stay away, but Setanta turned this warning into a challenge and took them all on at once, fighting with only his toy weapons.

One hundred and fifty javelins were thrown at him, but, deploying his toy shield, he made sure that none found their mark. Then, of the one hundred and fifty balls that were cast at him, he managed to thrust them all away using only his chest. The one hundred and fifty hurley sticks that were thrown did not touch him save for those he caught with one arm behind his back. To see him in his combat would have been to see a blur of golden light, so quickly were those toy weapons wielded. His movements flashed and spun until he was wrapped in a web of gold and it seemed to any onlooker that the sun itself was among them. It was then that his battle fury came upon him and with it every hair disappeared into his head as it swelled up with rage. Where each hair had been there were now fiery sparks. Beneath this fiery helmet his face became so distorted that one eye became as tiny as that of a needle and the other became as large as a bowl. His gape was so wide that his teeth looked to split his head in half from ear to ear and the inside of his throat was visible. Then he threw himself on fifty of his assailants and laid them low. Some ran for help to the chief, who was sitting at his board game. The boys jumped over both him and the table to escape Setanta, who was chasing them. When Setanta too jumped after them, the chief caught him and reprimanded him for his rough treatment of the boys.

Then the child complained at his own treatment, saying that he had left his mummy and daddy to play with them and they had been unwelcoming. When asked who his parents were, his answer revealed that he and the chief were closely related and that Setanta had the right to expect a better reception. The misunderstanding about not following the boys' custom of asking for protection was explained and the chief offered Setanta his instead. However, within the same day there was more disruption and when the chief asked why the arguing continued, Setanta insisted that it should be he who was made the boys' protector. After his previous display, it could hardly be argued that he didn't have the skill. It would be far better to have such a one for your protector than your enemy.

Not long after, Setanta's guardian was invited to a feast. As was his custom, the chief always said farewell to the boy warriors before he left on a journey, so he visited the training ground. There Setanta was showing off again, playing ball against one hundred and fifty of the older boys. They could not prevent him from getting his ball into their goal no matter how hard or often they tried, but he was always able to defend his goal against all of theirs. At wrestling the same numbers were repeated; he could throw all one hundred and fifty of them at once, but all of their combined strength could not prevail against his single power. When they played the game of stealing clothes, he was able to strip them naked, but not so much as his cloak pin was taken from him.

The chieftain was so delighted at this display that he invited the child to come with him to the feast. Setanta replied that he still wanted to play and that he would follow him later, so the old man left without him and made his way with a few companions to his host, who was Cuillain the Smith. When they had arrived, Cuillain asked whether any more guests were coming, but by now the old chief had forgotten about Setanta and told his host that they were all here. Then Cuillain said that he would let his watchdog loose while they were all safe inside, to guard his flocks and herds. This dog was so huge and strong that it could only be controlled by three men holding on to its three chains.

Setanta finally made his way to the smith's feast, making the journey shorter in his favourite fashion – throwing his javelin and catching it before it could fall. He was still playing when the hound attacked him. Everyone in the smith's hall could hear the encounter and the chief cried out in anguish when he realised who was being savaged. Everyone knew that the child would be killed and the host's people were terrified of the retribution that would be visited on those who were responsible for the death of an heir to the leadership of the tribe. However, their fear was misplaced as Sctanta had already killed the hound with his bare hands. Welcoming him with both traditional courtesy and relief, Cuillain the Smith also said what an unfortunate feast it had been for himself, his lands and his people. That hound had been like a trusted man of the family, to be relied upon to protect them and all their wealth – he did not know how they would manage without him.

Setanta replied that it was of no importance because he would train a puppy of the same stock to replace the hound that he had killed. Furthermore, in the meantime, he himself would be the smith's protector, and just like that dog, he would ensure the safety of all the smith's livestock. Then one of the company said that from that moment he should be known as Cu Chullainn, which means 'Chullain's Hound'. The child objected to this and wanted to keep his original name, but for that one deed and for his reputation as a protector that he himself had forged, he was known as Cu Chullain for evermore.

SONS OF THE EARTH GODDESS

Knowest thou where should be
The night waiting the passing of the day?
Knowest thou a sign,
How many leaves there are?
Who uplifted the mountain,
Before the elements fell?
Who supports the structure
Of the earth for a habitation? ...

The Book of Taliesin

For a goddess to have given birth to a silent, stupid, hideous child had never been known. It was a mystery. Afagddu never noticed the eyes that turned away from his misshaping, never heard any comments about him, never responded to anything that happened around him. He was as dull as he was ugly and as ugly as he was dull. It was as though he was casting only his shadow into this world while his soul was in quite another. His mother was determined to shed light onto this mystery – to force an entry into her son's Other World, which had been denied to her.

Ceridwen was an Earth goddess whose gifts were among the most prized among mortals. She was the one whose powers made our world teem with animal life. Goddess of Fertility, her symbol was the sow, that creature known for her huge and frequent litters. She had given the gift of pigs to a Welsh lord, a reward for his trust, tried and tested. They had issued from Mother Earth's great belly, through the tunnel that led from the Underworld into ours – which had not yet seen such an animal, a most delicious food, generous in offspring and able to sustain itself on almost anything.

Deep in the womb of the Earth, Ceridwen tended the Cauldron of Inspiration. Potions brewed in that magical vessel could imbue poets with fiery inspiration, make fools speak sense and children speak wisdom to make their elders wonder. She decided to use it to bring Afagddu the power of speech, to enable him to utter wise words about that world which was mere darkness to her and to shed light on what it contained.

To do this she would bring the Cauldron of Inspiration to our world, where she would find the profusion of herbs and plants that she had given us long ago. From these she would distil the magical infusion to bring her son speech and wisdom. She would turn his blighted existence into one of eloquence – and the knowledge she would glean from his other world would add to the power she deployed in hers. So it was that she stayed longer among mortals than was her wont, bringing all she needed from the Underworld to be able to cast her magic in this one. It would take a year and a day just to gather the plants she needed, each one according to the particular phase of the moon that ensured it was at its most potent when gathered. And so she set to work.

She had a servant who was completely loyal to her, but his faithfulness was born of fear as Ceridwen had blinded him lest he read any of her spells or see the magical passes and gestures that accompanied them. So ruthless was the goddess in keeping her powers under her own control. Though loyal, the old man's abilities were limited due to his blindness, and she would need more help. The magical infusion would need to be kept at a constant temperature, between simmering and boiling, and no part of it could be allowed to stick to the cauldron's sides. Moreover, this had to be maintained for a year and a day, and it would take a younger person's energy and keen sight to accomplish the task: the potion would need to be stirred ceaselessly for all that time. The servant was sent to the nearest settlement to find such a one among the village children, who scattered as soon as they saw him. They too knew the story of who blinded him and feared anything or anybody to do with his mistress. There was only one who did not run away, Little Gwion, the smallest of them all, undersized and in all ways immature for his age. He was an easy catch even for the old man, and soon found himself deep in the woods under Ceridwen's orders.

Day after day, night after night, Little Gwion stirred to keep Agfaddu's cure at a constant temperature, blended and quickening to potency. It was as though his puny arms moved in rhythm to his dreams, for surely he slept at times, even continuing his task in his sleep for fear of his new mistress. As for the goddess, she was ceaselessly busy elsewhere on this, our Earth, Ceridwen's charge and creation. It was her touch that turned the green of summer's leaf into the first gold glints of autumn, her sharp glance that wakened the first frosts, her scented breath that burst buds into blossom, her gentle gaze that turned summer seas into shimmering blue. The wheel of the year had turned full circle and it was only a matter of a few hours before her magical infusion would be ready for the unreachable son living in utter darkness. So it was that the spiral of her spell drew her back towards the fire that had never been allowed to fail.

Now that the potion seethed with its gathering power, Little Gwion became even drowsier over its fumes. Three bubbles appeared on its glossy surface; three bubbles that burst and spat. The burning liquid landed on Little Gwion's hand. Instinctively he put his hand to his mouth to soothe it with his tongue. As he sucked at the pain, those three drops trickled down his throat, sweeter than honey, stronger than wine, weightier than all the rooted trees of the forest. Behind his eyelids, still screwed up with the shock of the pain, Little Gwion could already see all that had been, all that was happening now and all that was to come. He understood why the tides turn and why the moon waxes and wanes. He saw where the geese went in the winter and how the caterpillar becomes a butterfly. He knew why mens' hair turns white and why their beards turn first. He was certain that a woman will not look at the man she desires while a man will look at nothing else. But beneath this great swell of knowledge ran the presence of something else – a wave of hatred was gathering to burst upon him – a wave of fury and revenge that now that Ceridwen's plan had been thwarted because he had swallowed the cure that was intended for her own son.

They say that thought is the fastest thing in the world – but for one who has consumed a divine elixir, magic is quicker. Faster than thought, Little Gwion knew that Ceridwen was coming for him with murder in her heart. Faster than thought, he used his new powers and shape-shifted himself into a hare. Now it was a hare, leaping from its form, that zigzagged its way from danger. However, it was soon followed by a greyhound as Ceridwen changed her shape in pursuit. At last, knowing that he was tiring and that the greyhound would soon be upon him, Little Gwion threw himself into the river, where he turned himself into a fish to hide beneath the water and swim from danger. If you had been there you would have seen a salmon diving and wondered at not first seeing it leap. But the all-seeing goddess had transformed herself into an otter and they became two streamlined shapes darting, twisting this way and that beneath the water. The otter was gaining on his salmon self and Little Gwion knew he would be caught at her next lunge, so he jumped from the water and in mid salmon leap, shape-shifted himself into a swallow and flew high into the sky. No matter how far this swallow flew there was now a hawk above, first poised then stooping. Time and time again the swallow just managed to avoid those talons, but all the hawk had to do was hover from a greater height while the swallow swooped and twirled and grew tired. Then at last, far below, the swallow saw a threshing floor heaped with grain. A final stretch of flight and Little Gwion had changed himself from swallow to a grain of corn. There he lay, hidden in plain sight among many of his kind, still and at rest. But with hawk's eyes Ceridwen had seen from her great height exactly which grain Little Gwion had become. She swooped for a last time and as the hawk's talons touched the threshing floor she became a black hen and gobbled the grain that the boy had become.

There was a glitter of triumph in the hen's beady eye and a blaze of victory in the eyes of the goddess as Ceridwen regained her form. She had caught and consumed that little sneak thief who had stolen her son's destiny, and now he had paid for his transgression with his life. But Little Gwion had consumed something of the goddess herself, something of the power that had gone into the strongest spell of her own making. The divine magic that was inside him could not be snuffed out. He was no longer entirely mortal. Cell by cell it grew, until by the swelling of her belly Ceridwen knew that she was pregnant with a different kind of seed and that the destiny that Little Gwion had stolen had now become part of her own. Yet within the weave of every fate there appear to be choices, and she decided to destroy the child as soon as it was born. When that time came, she took the baby between her two hands to crush the life out of him once and for all. But as she held him, she saw a child so wondrously beautiful that she was unable to destroy him. Instead she wrapped him in a leather bag and placed him on the waters of the river where he had first tried to escape her. So it was that she allowed Little Gwion to at last be swept away into the tide of his own destiny.

2

Tales of Magic, Enchantment and Trickery

Merlin's Prophecy

Now that he was deemed the wisest in the land, Britain became known as 'Merlin's Bounds' – as though it were Merlin who decided what should flourish within or be banished. It was time for his prophecy about the red and white dragons to unfurl into truth – and the first part of that prophecy was for the Saxon usurpers to be routed. Two brothers, Aurelius the elder, and Uther, rightful heirs to British kingship, returned from their exile in Brittany where, fleeing from their Cornish home, they had sought asylum as children. Their return was welcomed by Merlin, who some believed was their nephew. Many Britons flocked to the standard of the Cornish Boar, and those who remembered Merlin's prophecy made sure that it was repeated far and wide. Together the brothers would succeed in destroying Vortigern and his son.

As Uther was on his way to fight a decisive battle, he saw, emblazoned across the sky, a scarlet comet shaped like a dragon. Merlin's interpretation of this omen was that the time of the red dragon had come, but that it would be the younger brother, Uther, who would rule. So Uther caused a dragon standard to be made and became known by the title of Uther 'Pendragon'. Merlin's prophecy soon came true, as Aurelius was discovered to have been treacherously killed, murdered by poisoning. Merlin then created a fitting monument for Aurelius' tomb, the mighty structure we now call Stonehenge, its very shape a prophecy of the Round Table yet to come. So it was that Uther Pendragon became king and was indebted to Merlin for his prophecies – or did he also believe that Merlin's magic had caused all this to come about?

The outside enemy had been defeated, but what of its legacy – the enemy within, fuelled by the constant feuding and fighting between the British themselves. They would have to be united under one ruler, and he had not yet been born.

Uther's first task was to secure Merlin's Bounds to its furthest borders and he was aided in this by Gorlois of Cornwall. Gorlois, who not so long ago, in this fractured, faction-led country had once been an enemy, was now an ally. At last, one of their campaigns led to the far west and when the fighting was finally over, they found themselves at Gorlois' castle, Dimilioc in Cornwall. How good it was to be able to trust one's companions, to sheath one's sword in a place where the rise and fall of war clamour had given way to the steady pulse of the westerly wind from the ocean.

As they drew close, the castle lay crouched against the darkening horizon, but suddenly warm light spilled out into the dusk, bringing with it the noise of busyness and greetings. The war party had arrived with their long absent lord and the country's new king. Somehow Merlin had preceded them, so all was ready for welcomes and feasting. He drew back as the ladies hastened towards long-awaited families, husbands and honoured guests.

The feasting progressed in a glorious procession of colour and music and flavours long forgotten by fighting men who were always on the move. Rare wines loosened tongues and delicious food loosened belts. After many months of campaigning, Uther allowed himself to imagine a peaceful land – one where crops flourished into harvests and where birdsong could be heard more often than the clash of weapons. Was it the feeling of relief at battles closely won, or the sweet, unaccustomed wine that stroked this gentle reverie into a dream state, one in which the sound and colour of the feasting hall receded and his immediate field of vision filled his whole world?

The crimson silken sleeve before him was sleeker than any rose petal, its colour more vibrant than any he had ever seen. His eyes pricked with tears at its intensity. The dragon-shaped comet, if he had been capable of remembering it, would have paled by comparison. But Uther was incapable of remembering anything, who or where he was or even why he had come to this place. He was like an insect caught between the glistening scarlet jaws of the sundew plants that grew so profusely in the boggy moorland around the castle. An insect trapped by beauty, sinking oblivious towards its fate, fuel for another purpose. The sleeve was closer now, its scent so sweetly pervasive that its fragrance reached deep into his heart, twisting it like a skilful hand plucking a thorny rose. And then there was the hand itself, blooming from beneath the sleeve, and Uther knew that nowhere in the whole wide world would be found a hand as exquisite as that one. Fascinated, he watched as it seemed to make passes across his line of vision, which he was as unable to shift as was the banqueting hall to detach itself and sail through the air like a boat. Shimmering skin and pearly nails appeared and retreated beneath the crimson cloth, each fold and crease of skin, each whorl of knuckle lovelier than any valley or hill in Paradise. Then at last he blinked and his gaze shifted. He was looking at his hostess' hand refilling his drinking horn. He looked up into the face of Gorlois' wife Igraine, but even before their eyes met it was too late, he was in love – in love with the kind of passion that no mortal is fit to endure for long – and as their eyes met, Igraine could see it.

Uther was High King, he could have had any unmarried woman in the land – princess, commoner or slave – but at that moment he knew that there was no other he wanted and Igraine knew it too. That fatal moment, as the spell was set, was noticed by yet another whose blood ran with magic, for how would she not sense that which stirred her own powers? Igraine's daughter, Morgause, was one in whom the old blood ran strong. Sorceress, priestess of the old religion, some said that she and others in her line were descended from the goddess whose influence still bound the destiny of the land. Quick as a falcon in flight, Morgause's eyes swooped around the room until they stooped on Merlin. There he stood, his eyes glittering with intent, his lips still shaping that silent spell. Morgause knew from that moment that her gifts might one day be joined with his or pitted against them – and all this would be tested in some distant time by her brother who was yet to be born, but whose fate lay already cradled in this web of magic, its strands still gleaming, newly woven as they were from Merlin's mouth.

It was all that Igraine could do to steady her pitcher of wine rather than spill it. There she sat at Uther's right hand, desperately hoping that nobody would notice that he only had eyes for her, that he had ceased eating or drinking and that his face was always turned in her direction. As soon as she could she slipped away, feeling her king's hot gaze upon her back. She sent a servant to her husband with a message to meet her in her chamber. There she told him that she would not be safe in Uther's company, that he meant to have her whether she was married to his greatest ally or not. Gorlois made secret preparations to take Igraine to his castle at Tintagel, an impregnable fortress only reachable by a narrow causeway and otherwise surrounded by the sea. The only danger at Tintagel was from the raging tides as they hurled themselves at the granite fangs of the cliffs or crept up on the unwary, trapping them on some distant strand. A few men could hold it against many and it was a place where Uther could never reach her. There Igraine would be safe from his overriding lust.

Gorlois' servants were instructed to keep their departure hidden for as long as possible. They distracted the king with more food, minstrels, jugglers and tumblers, but always the king's eyes roamed desperately for Igraine. Merlin watched knowing that the longer this was drawn out the more pliable Uther would become in his thwarted rage. At last his hosts' flight was discovered and passion consumed the king, who had counted on getting Igraine into his bed that very night. This was a turn of events that Merlin knew how to use to his advantage and he advised Uther to accuse them of treachery – disappearing without his leave, abandoning him far from his own court and army. Was the plan to ambush him and seize power themselves? He should lose no time in gaining the upper hand and declaring war on Gorlois. Then Merlin revealed the rest of his plan: when Gorlois had been drawn out from Tintagel to engage with Uther's forces in enmity once more, Merlin would use his art to change Uther's shape into that of

Gorlois. Magic would ensure that nobody, not even Igraine, would be able to tell him apart from her true husband. She would then take him into her bed believing that her victorious husband, her protector, had returned triumphant from battle. Such was Uther's overwhelming passion that he never for a moment questioned the wisdom of turning his hard-won ally into an enemy once more.

'What would I do without you, Merlin, my dearest friend! How understanding you are even though you seem never to seek the company of women yourself. Would you do all this for me?'

'A small thing to do for my king – but they do say that you get nothing for nothing, there is always a price to pay, especially when dealing with the "other" arts. It would be unchancy to forget that.'

'No price would be too great, my mage, name it.'

'There will be a son conceived this night. You must promise him to me. I will take him as soon as he is born and, for his own protection, he will be raised without knowing who his real parents are. There will come a time when he will know who he is and what his destiny.'

But Uther was not thinking of any consequences. Spellbound, he agreed and gave Merlin his promise. All came to pass just as the magician had said. The baby was taken soon after his birth from a mother who had been deceived by her king and widowed by him in the same night. Then she endured the loss of her only son. Her daughter, Morgause, saw all that happened, the old magic straining in her blood, seeking action. But like a hunter holding taught the leashes of the pack when the quarry has been sighted, she held back until the years of watching and divining would reveal a path that she, too, could shape.

The baby boy was Prince Arthur, fated to become the greatest king this island has ever known. He had no idea of what awaited him as he grew up, unknowingly fostered by a kindly knight and his lady and an overbearing older brother. From time to time an avuncular old man would visit the family, an old friend of his father's, or so Arthur thought. It was once again Merlin's magic that ensured that only Arthur, while still a boy, would be the only one among the knights of the realm to be able to pull a sword from a stone, thus proving his inheritance and the right to be High King within Merlin's Bounds.

ENCHANTING THOR'S WOUND

There was not much that would attract a giant's notice unless it was something precious, and even more so if it belonged to someone else. On this occasion it was a flash of gold from the helmet worn by Odin, All Father, God of War. There he was, galloping past between the world of the goddesses and gods and the world of the giants, riding his eight-legged steed, Sleipnir. It was the chief of the stone giants, Hrungnir, who had noticed his divine counterpart speed by. Until then Hrungnir had believed his own mount to be the fastest of horses even if he only had four legs to match Sleipnir's eight and even though he had to bear the weight of his master, who was made entirely of stone. The giant bellowed to Odin to stop and, mounting Goldenmane, he galloped after him. When the giant declared that Goldenmane was the faster of the two, Odin laughed and made a comment that was the equivalent of, 'Over my dead body!'

At this Hrungnir had been given another incentive for proving that his mount was the faster. Apart from the glory in proving that his horse was the best in all the worlds, Odin's throwaway bet meant that he would have to forfeit his life when Goldenmane won. The race of gods and goddesses had made enemies of the giants since time was new – what rejoicing there would be in the land of the giants when his subjects learned that he had bested the most powerful of their eternal foes. The race began, and the steeds were well matched. The course was long and fast, and they headed straight for Asgard, the realm of the gods and goddesses. Too late Odin realised that Sleipnir was going too fast to turn and was heading straight for its wall at literally breakneck speed. Both mounts gave a mighty leap and jumped right over it. Now there was a giant, bitter enemy of the gods, at the heart of their realm.

Giant or not, the law of hospitality applied and Hrungnir feasted with the gods and goddesses – but it was the goddesses he was most interested in. Soon he was so drunk that he threatened to relocate Valhalla, Odin's feasting hall for dead warriors, to the realm of the giants. Then he was going to kill all the gods and goddesses except for Freya, Odin's consort, and Sif, Thor's wife, who he would spare so that they could become his mistresses. Guest or no guest, he would have to be dealt with and Thor, mightiest fighter of all, was sent for. But Thor was already on the case and dragged him outside, for which insult he was challenged to a duel.

This was going to cause so much damage that Thor insisted that it happened in the giant's world. When the appointed hour came, the adversaries each brought their seconds. The giant's consisted of a vast creature made of earth whose head touched the sky and whose girth equalled a copse of mature oak trees.

As Thor thundered towards his foe, he left a wake of earthquakes and avalanches, and underground fires rushed ahead of him. These alone put fear into the giants as their world was made of frost and ice. Before Thor was even close enough to throw his war hammer, Mjolnir, the giant's enormous companion had wet himself with fear and was to be laid low by a single blow, delivered by Thor's second. Made of clay from a river that bordered their world, he crumbled back into the element from which he had been made. The stone giant's weapon was unsurprisingly also made of stone – he fought with a whetstone, shaped from a meteorite, that only he could lift. The enemies hurled their weapons at each other from afar. Whetstone and hammer collided in mid-air, stone on iron, iron on stone. Mjolnir broke the whetstone into many fragments, which mortals find and use to hone their tools to this day, but one of these pieces lodged itself in Thor's skull. His hammer continued on its journey, killed the giant and returned to Thor's hand as it always did when thrown in battle. The dead giant then toppled over, pinning Thor to the ground with his stone leg.

Nobody was able to release him, until, at last, his son arrived, who was only 3 years old and whose mother was a giantess. He freed his father easily, and, much to Odin's covetous displeasure, was given Goldenmane as a reward. Honour was avenged and the giants had been taught a lesson. Thor returned triumphantly to the realm of the gods. On his way home he released one of the giant's prisoners and carried him back in a basket. However, despite returning in triumph, he still had the piece of whetstone lodged in his forehead. No great beauty to begin with, Thor did not appreciate how it marred his profile and was also concerned that it might interfere with his aim when he threw Mjolnir.

Help was at hand, however, in the form of Groa, a sorceress and healer of whom it was said that all things could be charmed at the sound of her voice. First she pointed her magic staff at him, then she began to sing. Such was her craft that no other stony item in the realm of the goddesses and gods responded, otherwise they would have been crushed by the mighty giant-built stone wall that surrounded the divine realm of Asgard – it was only the whetstone that moved. Thor felt it gradually twisting, deep inside his forehead, like a very gentle screw, as it listened to Groa's enchanting voice. Delighted at feeling it stir, the ever impulsive Thor burst out his thanks by telling Groa that it was her husband, Orvandill, whom he had released from the giant's imprisonment. But sorceresses, like storytellers, should never be interrupted. The overjoyed Groa stopped singing, and the whetstone sherd stopped moving. Carried away on the crest of his enthusiasm, Thor continued to tell Groa that unfortunately one of Orvandill's toes had been sticking out of the weave of the carrying basket and become frostbitten. Feeling remorse at this, Thor had snapped it off and flung it into the sky where it had become a star.

At that news, the enchantress became so enchanted herself that she was unable to complete her spell. Magic, once disrupted is never quite the same. To start the spell again would have been to take too much of a risk, especially with one whose head injury could have threatened what wasn't a very large brain to begin with. So the piece of whetstone remained in Thor's forehead forever, although, as it had already started to twist, we can hope that it wasn't so noticeable when in profile. As for her husband's toe, it stayed shining in the heavens forever, and there, giants, goddesses, gods and people still call the evening star by the name of Orvandill.

SHINING BROW, SILVER TONGUE

Sons do not always resemble fathers, nor fathers their sons. All his life, Elphin had been the unluckiest of men. It was as though he had been cursed, but nobody knew why or how. His father,

Gwyddno, was a great lord with rich lands and a splendid city. He had long ago given up sighing at the latest misadventure of his boy. Better to save his breath, or he was like to die for lack of it, if he sighed at each misfortune in the continuous sad procession that was Elphin's life.

Each year, at the blessed feast of Beltane it was the custom to lay nets and fish traps at the place where the river met the sea. Overnight the tide would not fail to bring in such bounty that the money from the sale of salmon filled the lord's treasury. At first light on the 1st May, for the first time, Elphin decided to be among the young people who went to gather in the sea's harvest. But on this May morning things were different. The nets that should have been thrashing with salmon were hanging empty and flaccid. There wasn't a fish to be seen. Elphin's companions began to mutter among themselves,

'Is it because *he* is with us that the nets are empty?'

'How could the salmon know that Elphin would be coming this year when he never has before?'

'With *his* luck, the biggest catch ever could have got away no matter how strong the nets.'

'*His* luck could make them fly clean away and back to the sea.'

The group stared in dismay. What were they going to tell their lord?

'But look, there is something!' cried Elphin.

His companions sniggered as he waded out to where a sodden leather bag lay caught in the branches that held a net. This he detached and brought back to the shore.

'Best let someone else open it – no need to turn any treasure to pebbles at your touch!'

The cruellest joined in with the joke, but Elphin was already opening the bag. As soon as his fingers had touched it, he felt them glowing with a strange warmth. It spread up his arms and seemed to fill his whole body with a gentle glow. Elphin knew that from this moment his life would be changed forever. No need to respond to the boys' mockery, it was now meaningless. His eager fingers plucked at the stitching around the bag, it fell open and at once he turned away, dazzled. The others shielded their eyes at the golden blaze of light that rivalled the day's new sun. Squinting, they saw Elphin holding an exquisite baby boy, his forehead shining with a brilliant light.

'Taliesin, I will call you, my beautiful boy, Taliesin of the shining brow, so you will be known and so remembered.'

But now it was the baby's turn to speak. He gazed at the one who had freed him from his leather prison in which he had floated alone for many years. Although still a tiny child, his speech was perfect, and his eloquence beyond the reach of any mortal:

Never in Gwyddno's weir
Was there such good luck as this night.
Fair Elphin, dry thy cheeks!
Being too sad will not avail.
Although thou thinkest thou hast no gain,
Too much grief will bring thee no good;
Nor doubt the miracles of the Almighty:
Although I am but little, I am highly gifted.
From seas, and from mountains,
And from the depths of rivers,
God brings wealth to the fortunate man ...
Weak and small as I am,
On the foaming beach of the ocean,
In the day of trouble I shall be
Of more service to thee than three hundred salmon.

Elphin of notable qualities,
Be not displeased at thy misfortune;
Although reclined thus weak in my bag,
There lies a virtue in my tongue.
While I continue thy protector
Thou hast not much to fear …

Elphin did not know whether he was dreaming or whether he had simply gone mad and could not trust his own senses. He gaped at the baby like one of the fish he had expected to be in the net. Feeling like a fish out of water would have been an understatement. Fortunately his companions from his father's court were there, too. They too were sharing everything he had seen and heard.

'My radiant boy, who are you and where have you come from?' he stammered.

I have been in a multitude of shapes,
Before I assumed a consistent form.
I have been a sword, narrow, variegated …
I have been a tear in the air,
I have been the dullest of stars.
I have been a word among letters,
I have been a book in the origin.
I have been the light of lanterns,
A year and a half.
I have been a continuing bridge,
Over three score estuaries.
I have been a course, I have been an eagle.
I have been a coracle in the seas:
I have been compliant in the banquet.
I have been a drop in a shower;

I have been a sword in the grasp of the hand
I have been a shield in battle.
I have been a string in a harp,
Disguised for nine years.
in water, in foam.[1]

Elphin took Taliesin home to his father's court and from that day delighted in his foster son. And it was true that his luck had changed. He barely knew a day of misfortune. Gwyddno died a happier man knowing that finding Taliesin had changed his son's life to the good at last. In time, Elphin married and all was peace and happiness in their home until he was called away to a feast to which the king of the country had summoned all his nobles.

King Maelgwyn kept a sumptuous court where every luxury of the day could be found. However, his greatest joy and the one for which he was most renowned was his coterie of bards. Surely his chief bard was the most accomplished in all the land of Wales, not to mention his entourage of apprentices that could soon rival him in fluency, wit and eloquence. Of course, such a feast, lasting as it did for many days, served to keep an eye on the lords in his region. It was also an ideal opportunity to show off the talent of his bards. That and the horse racing that was to follow would provide the best entertainment in the whole country.

Elphin had never been to Maelgwyn's court. Perhaps because of his unchancy youth, his father had not dared to introduce him to such a powerful ruler. Elphin was nervous about attending such a grand event, and he decided to make himself less conspicuous by travelling alone. Maelgwin was no fool, he knew that retaining power depended on a thorough knowledge

1   *The Book of Taliesin.*

58

of the elite that surrounded him. Here was a newcomer and he meant to sound him out. However, to calm his nerves, Elphin had drunk rather more than was wise. The wine had led him from one extreme to another as he relaxed into a brash cocksure confidence without realising it. When invited to praise the virtue of Maelgwyn's queen, the prowess of the king's bards and the quality of his horseflesh, his reply brought silence to the banqueting hall.

'Sire, your wife may be virtuous, who am I to say, but I can tell you that of all the ladies in the land, it is my own wife who is the most virtuous. As for your bards, however talented they may be, without a doubt my own could surpass all of them put together. As for your horses, well, the very least of mine could beat them in a race.'

The silence that followed those rash and insulting words was like a mounting wave that threatened to crush all beneath its breaking. Maelgwyn's face was as dark as the storm that had drawn such a wave from the depth of anger. But he was a wise ruler and powerful. Why would he need to lose control? In a voice as quiet and steady as the breeze that fills the sails of the vessel of good fortune, he replied, 'Boastful and insulting are you words, newcomer Elphin, son of my old friend Gwyddno. Perhaps your old reputation is livelier than recent reports to speak so unwisely. Boastful are your words as my prison bars are strong, and it is there that you will stay while the virtue of your wife is tested.'

The king's guard led Elphin to the dungeons and the king ordered that his own son, Rhun, be sent to Elphin's home to test his wife's virtue. This plan was as clever as it was vengeful, for Rhun also had a reputation – that of a womaniser. The more charitable said that no woman could resist him, but perhaps those who said that he took what he wanted if it was not given willingly, were closer to the truth. In those days, in that place, as it still is in some to this day, a woman's virtue was considered worthless even if she had not consented to such an act – the fact that it had happened was enough. The king gave Rhun a ring of great value with which to bribe Elphin's wife. Once it was on her finger, he was to chop it off and bring it back to his father as proof.

Elphin, already imprisoned, knew nothing of this plan, but Taliesin did. As soon as those foolish words were leaving his foster father's mouth the bard knew the danger. With his inner scrying eye he could see all that had happened, and the king's unfolding plot against his foster family. He then told his foster mother to exchange clothes with a kitchen maid and to dress the maid in the finest of garments and jewels. He assured the maid that she would be recompensed for whatever she might lose. When Rhun arrived he was made welcome and he greeted the kitchen maid as the lady of the house, never suspecting that she was in disguise. However, a 'maid' and a youth would never leave her side and even Rhun was having difficulty in perpetrating the next phase of his father's plan. However, he did not dare return to court without having accomplished it. He needed that finger with the ring upon it, and who in his father's distant court would know what had or hadn't passed between them? In the end he pretended to offer the ring freely as a gift from his father and placed it on the maid's hand, still believing that it was her mistress'. The maid didn't have time to admire it. Rhun's dagger was out of its sheath and in a moment there was a bloody round wound where her finger had been – and the king's son was galloping back with his trophy.

Taliesin followed him on the best of Elphin's remaining horses. He was there when Elphin was dragged from prison, overjoyed to see Taliesin, knowing that now help was at hand, quite literally, as the king dangled the bloodied finger, still wearing the ring in front of him. It was as though Taliesin's wisdom was putting the very words in his mind to utter. Elphin glanced his way and saw the youth, unnoticed, leaning against the wall. Only Elphin saw that the lad's lips were moving, silently speaking into his mind whatever he should say next. Then he heard his own voice speaking again without forethought to the king, but this time with better effect.

'If it please you Sire, let me see that finger.'

Maelgwyn wondered what difference that would make and how this fool proposed to wriggle out of the situation. But he needed to be seen to be magnanimous and assented.

Elphin handled the finger and almost smiled as he said, 'Not my wife's ring, indeed, Sire, perhaps yours, however, this is not my wife's finger. See how ill-fitting it is. My wife's fingers are more slender, this looks to be thickened by rough work. See how the ring is cutting into it. Also, my wife's habit is to be meticulous at her toilette, cutting her nails at the full and the new moon. This nail is too long for that.'

Again the court was silenced, but this time at his good sense. How different was his speech when wine was not talking, and nobody knew that it was the youth's words speaking through the terrified Elphin. But he hadn't finished:

'If you look carefully beneath the nail, Sire, you will see that there is dough beneath it. Rye dough, I believe. My lady has servants to do such work, she does not need to knead dough herself.'

There was almost a titter in the court as Taliesin could not restrain himself from putting that pun into Elphin's mouth despite the danger that he was in.

Maelgwyn snatched back the finger and pocketed the ring. His sharp eyes sought out Rhun, lurking in a shadowy corner, to be dealt with later. But there was still the matter of the insult to his bards and his captive was returned to prison, still wearing his chains of silver – such was his right as a nobleman – but chains nevertheless, there to languish unless his boast could be proved. It was not long before the bardic contest took place. Everyone knew who would win, but everyone also wanted to listen to the magnificent offerings that would be heard during this most exalted of event in this celebration of the oral arts. Some of the listeners, bards themselves, also knew that however low or high they might be ranked, they would at least be heard as they took their turn among the great.

Then a cruel and strange thing happened to each and every one who tried. As each bard stood on the dais, instead of reciting their compositions of exquisite poetry, gibberish poured from their mouths. The kind of nonsense sounds that would at first make a nursemaid smile at her infant charge, and that would soon tire any parent. At first nobody noticed the youth standing in the corner, his index finger playing his pouting lips at speed so that the only words that could escape from the bard's mouths were meaningless blurs. Maelgwyn was outraged. Did not every noble's reputation also depend on that of their bard? What was this mockery? At last his chief bard managed to gesture to the young man nobody had noticed before, and gasp out that it was he who was putting a spell on them all. At that Taliesin stepped forward and, announcing himself as Elphin's bard, he proclaimed:

> I am a harmonious one; I am a clear singer.
> I am steel; I am a druid.
> I am an artificer; I am a scientific one.
> I am a serpent; I am love; I will indulge in feasting.
> I am not a confused bard drivelling,
> When songsters sing a song by memory

I am not a mute artist,
Conspicuous among the bards of the people.
I animate the bold,
I influence the heedless;
I wake up the looker on,
The enlightener of bold kings.
I am not a shallow artist,
Conspicuous among kindred bards …

He demanded that Elphin be released from prison but Maelgwyn was too furious at being bested by a boy to give the order.

'Let us have more entertainment then. Who can answer me this riddle?

Created before the deluge.
A creature strong,
Without flesh, without bone,
Without veins, without blood,
Without head, and without feet.
It will not be older, it will not be younger,
Than it was in the beginning.'

There are few bards who can resist trying to solve a riddle, but before anyone in that company could reply, Taliesin summoned the answer so that it sprang towards them. The wind slammed open the door and, like a giant hand, tore all the cloths and furnishings from where they hung. Next it flung all that was laid on the banqueting table around the room. Goblets and flagons, platters and food ricocheted off the walls. Then people were lifted into the air, crushed against the ceiling, hurled out of doors and windows. They clutched at each other in their panic, hand torn from hand, garments ripping, crying out in fear.

'Release Elphin! Bring him forth!' shouted the king.

When he stood before him, a few words from Taliesin cracked the silver chains that bound him. But Maelgwyn would not give up, he knew that he owned the best horses in the land and he was determined that he would be proved right at least in this.

The race was to happen the following day on the beach at low tide, its course to circle the strand three times. Twenty-four of the very best of the king's horses were paraded before the crowd. Their magnificent heads nodded up and down as they paced, and their manes tossed as they pawed the ground in their eagerness. So magnificent were they that some said they were of the same blood as the white horses of the sea god Dylan himself. Taliesin, bard turned groom for the occasion, led out Elphin, who of course had no jockey with him. His mount was indifferent, being neither racer nor charger. The crowd soon ignored him as all eyes turned once more to the best display of horseflesh that they were ever likely to see again. But what they hadn't noticed was Taliesin whispering into the rider's ear and handing him twenty-four switches of burned holly brands, each one with a magical sign burnt into its bark. Even if they had noticed, they would not have been able to hear Taliesin's instructions: to touch each of the horses on the rump with one of the brands as they passed, and then to throw it ahead of them. At the end of the race he was to throw his cap up in the air and leave it upon the ground wherever it landed.

Compared to the others, it was as though Elphin was ambling along on his mount and would still have seemed to, even had it been at all inclined to make an effort. At that pace it was certain that the other horses would pass it as they repeated their circuits. As each one did so, Elphin whacked it on the rump with a holly brand and threw it in front of its rider. When each of these had landed on the ground, the horse refused to pass it. It was as though the riders were fighting with the sea itself as their mounts fought their bits, turned on the spot, reared and bucked and danced every which way except forward. By the time that all of them were under Taliesin's spell, Elphin's horse was barely trotting, and that was how he passed the finish. The winner was greeted with gales of laughter rather than rousing cheers. Remembering to throw his cap into the air, he watched as it soared like a swallow, like a hawk, as a youth ran like a streak of light beneath it, following its journey, until it fell to the silver sand at last.

Taliesin stood on that spot, commanding people to fetch spades and tools, to start digging before the place was swallowed by the incoming tide, and they ran to his bidding. Before long a great cauldron was revealed, containing silver treasure beyond any that had ever yet been seen, and other magical objects beyond the value of mere coinage. But everybody knew that by far the greatest treasure was the cauldron itself.

So it was that Elphin was allowed to return home in triumph and how good luck and increase attended him for the rest of his days. And as for Taliesin, that magical child of the Earth goddess Ceridwen, himself a divinity of inspiration and the arts, it is said that he attended many royal courts, whether in that time or other times. Bard even to the court of King Arthur, he spoke of his conversations with Merlin in Arianrhod's spinning sky palace, where she still lives, Goddess of the Silver Wheel of Destiny. Some even believed him to be an incarnation of Merlin himself. Whether you believe this or not, you can retrace his steps to this day. Where he passed in flight or stood his ground is forever remembered in the names of the Welsh landscape.

And before I desire the end of existence,
And before the broken foam shall come upon my lips,
And before I become connected with wooden boards,
May there be festivals to my soul!
Book-learning scarcely tells me
Of severe afflictions after death-bed;
And such as have heard my bardic books
They shall obtain the region of heaven …

LOST ON THE MOUNTAIN

Finn mac Cumhaill was the mightiest leader of warriors that Ireland had ever known. Captain of the Fianna, that band of heroes and heroines, it was their task to defend the shores of the realm. To join the Fianna it was not sufficient to be a great fighter, you were also required to be a hunter, musician, poet and storyteller, at the very least. And what tremendous tests you would have had to pass to join those talented people – such as running bent double under branches while removing a thorn from your foot without slackening pace or losing one word or beat of the song you were singing.

The greatest of all of these was Finn himself, who, as people said, was not purely mortal but also had divine blood in him. How else would it have been possible for his mother to hide him from his father's enemies before he was born? For twelve years she hid in a hollow oak tree while pregnant with him. For twelve years soldiers and sentries patrolled the forest where she was known to be hiding. It was only when they had given up their search that she allowed herself to go into labour. So it was that Finn was born with all the knowledge of the forest, which allowed him to also be the greatest among hunters. Wise and cunning beyond most, he had acquired the gift of second sight by accidentally sucking the thumb on which burning drops had spurted from the cauldron in which lay the Salmon of Knowledge. This allowed him to see into other worlds, and to know when beings from the fairy realm had entered ours.

On this day Finn had been hunting with three companions. One was his son, Oisin, whose mother was a fairy woman, another, Goil, an old enemy who was now a staunch ally, and the last, Diarmid, foster son of Aengus, the God of Love. Throughout the day the band had started no quarry and Finn knew this was unchancy. The forest was oddly quiet, no birds sang, no leaves or twigs rustled at the passing of animals and even the wind was silent in the branches.

Evening was drawing on and the companions wondered whether they should spend the night on the mountain without food or drink or whether they should make for home while there was still enough light. They decided on the latter when, out of nowhere, a thick mist descended. From the pricking of his magical thumb, Finn knew that this was no ordinary mist and that some enchantment had conjured it. Having blundered about for a while, they had to admit that they were utterly lost and all they knew, from the feel of the slope beneath their feet, was whether they were going up or down, although even this was so variable as to be useless as a guide.

Not even being able to see their hands in front of their faces, it was more than strange when a light appeared. Holding on to each other so that none would become separated, they made their way towards it and from its faint glow could make out that it was shining from some kind of shelter. Just as Finn was about to knock, the door opened and a merry old man beckoned them inside, 'Was it all night you were going to make us wait for you?

Well never mind, here you are at last, cold, wet and hungry and in the right place for all those and more to be mended.'

With relief, the companions tumbled inside to see a merry fire, a trestle table and a bleary-eyed old goat tied with a filthy rope to an iron ring in the wall. Soon they were warm again but realised that they were in no ordinary home when the old man wiped his hands in his long white beard and clapped them. At that a lovely young woman appeared who was so beautiful that she made all their previous lovers look ugly enough to make anyone's eyes smart if they but glanced at them. If the men had any wits left, they would have wondered at how she had appeared from nowhere, there being no other door. She smiled sweetly at her guests and ignored their foolish blushes. Suddenly she was gone, but reappeared with a beautiful cloth to cover the table, and enormous quantities of food and drink. Before she could invite the men to be seated, however, the old goat broke free from its rope and leaped onto the table, scattering food everywhere as he launched himself at a bowl of apples.

Finn ordered the most senior of his companions to grab the animal and tie him up. Goil sprang to do so, grabbing the goat by the horns, but was unable to move him by even a hair's breadth. Was this truly one of Ireland's greatest warriors? Disgusted, Finn ordered Oisin to do it, but he too was quite unable to shift the creature. Next Diarmid also failed at this simple task. All the while, the young woman smiled sweetly and the man twisted his hands in his long white beard with glee. With one bound Finn was on the table with his arms around the animal, but he couldn't budge him. Neither was he going to give up. He put shoulder to shoulder and shoved as hard as he could, while grabbing the goat's hoof. His face darkened, his teeth ground together and his breath came in gasps. At last he managed to lift the hoof a few inches from the floor, before collapsing in an exhausted heap. The old man cackled delightedly, grabbed the trailing rope and easily led the goat back to its ring where it was tied up, still munching the last of the apples. The young woman replenished the table, but despite drinking and eating well, the companions, ashamed of their weakness, were unusually quiet.

After the meal, bedding appeared from nowhere, and the fire was allowed to burn down until all was dark in the room. During the night each of the companions made their way to where the young woman was lying, hoping that she would permit them to share her bed, but she rejected all of them. Only the youngest, Diarmid, received a kiss from her on his forehead before she pushed him away. In the morning the room was empty and the men were about to sneak away quietly, having embarrassed themselves further at their hostess' rejection. But suddenly, there she was, smiling, with the old man beside her.

'Last night each one of you tried to have me, forgetting that you have all had me before. My name is Youth and you will never have me again.'

At that the old man cackled his approval and said, 'That old goat you were wrestling with is Death, and nobody can move him when he has made up his mind, except for you, Finn mac Cumhaill. You of all our heroes managed to shift him, albeit slightly, and that has never been done by any living man before. The wish of my heart on you and yours Finn mac Cumhaill for your strength and courage. And as for me, I am Youth's father, my name is Time, and I can shift all things.'

Then there was a clap of thunder and the companions found themselves alone on the mountainside in the morning sunshine. From that time on, Diarmid had a mark on his forehead where Youth had kissed him. It became known as 'Diarmid's love spot' and any woman who caught sight of it would fall in love with him. This was to cause him so much trouble that he needed to keep it covered and grew his hair long accordingly. But as for Finn mac Cumhaill, who shifted Death just for a moment, it is said of him that he has never completely died. How can he have done when he is remembered from those days to these in the stories we tell of him. Indeed, it is said that our world will end if ever a day passes when his deeds are not told.

3

Tales of Creation, Nature and Healing

The Cailleach, Old Woman of Power

Far to the west lies, or rather floats, the Green Isle of Youth. Whether it drifts with the Atlantic currents or chooses its journey, nobody knows. All along the western seaboard of Scotland, greenery testifies to its presence, even in winter. There flowers grow, far from the southern lands where you would normally find them, leaning towards that island where ageing is unknown. Mortals have seen it appear fleetingly from the sea mist or from clifftops on a clear day as it drifts along the coast or caresses the horizon, but none have ever managed to land on its emerald shore. It is there that The Cailleach, the Old Woman of Power, retreats when spring has arrived in our world.

Some say that she seeks refuge on the isle to regain her strength, worn out by many battles and at last defeated by her own son, Aengus, God of Spring and Love. His father was the sun himself, who bestowed on him the gift of everlasting youth. Each year, just before the spring equinox, Old Woman of Power needs to recover from her defeat and retreat to the island to drink from its well of eternal youth. Those healing waters send her into a deep sleep until the days grow short again. As she awakes and stretches, the tides rip and swell and her yawns and sighs become the gales of autumn.

However, wiser people know that these battles are merely a testing of her son's mettle. Old Woman needs to ensure that he has sufficient strength to bring forth the new growth of spring, and to sustain it throughout the ripening summer until after the harvest was brought in. That is why, at the end of winter, she drives Aengus away from the land again and again, back to the Isle of Youth, his winter home. At last she is satisfied by his efforts in resisting her, that the land and all upon it will be safe in his care.

Long, long before Aengus was born, when Time itself was new, the Old Woman of Power had set about creating the place we now call Scotland. Her only tools were her hammer and a creel woven from willow that she carried on her back. In this basket she carried any stones she might need with which to make the mountains. When she had dumped enough piles of these to the desired heights in the correct places, she smashed each of them into their distinctive shapes with her hammer. In this way the mountain ranges were created. When she banged her hammer on the ground, it froze. The more she banged, the deeper the frost grew and the wider it spread. Old Woman had made her country and her season, it was a place where winter flourished.

All this hard work had made her shawl dirty and it would need to be washed. Old Woman looked out over her newborn cliffs. There, between the western shore and the islands that had formed where she had thrown some spare boulders into the sea, was a good place to make her wash tub. She grabbed handfuls of seaweed from the shore and shoved them up one nostril to bring on a gigantic sneeze. The sneeze pushed the tide back towards Ireland, giving her enough time to work away at the seabed that would never otherwise have been exposed. She gouged out a deep trench and piled the scoopings up into a huge pillar. Using her hammer, she beat it into a tall pinnacle, aiming for smoothness – it wouldn't do get her clothes snagged on some rough stone. When she had been making the mountains she had been working with scale, now she was working with detail. Finally satisfied, she allowed herself a stretch and a yawn. The yawn drew the sea back as a towering great wave, rearing and thundering towards the shore. When it reached the reshaped seabed it created a massive whirlpool, which was perfect for washing Old Woman of Power's shawl. Beautifully clean, wrung out and hung out to dry on the highest mountains, it shone white as snow. It was the first snowfall. The whirlpool still remembers Old Woman's sneeze, which can be heard from miles away to this day in the roar it makes as the tide rushes in. When people see her shawl spread out on the mountains, they know that winter has settled in.

Old Woman of Power had created the landscape, the seasons and the weather. Her body, her moods and her spirit were all of these. The land and the life it sustained was the incarnation of herself. Old Mother Cailleach had created Nature with all her abounding life; she herself was Nature. As she walked about her sovereign land, bird and beast, flocks and herds, followed her. No need to succumb, therefore, to her invading son Aengus, only a need to make sure that he was fit to take on the guardianship of her beloved land, if only for a while.

Long, long before Aengus was born, Old Mother Cailleach had many other sons. In her act of creating the mountains, so potent was the life force in her great hands that even the boulders she had touched and discarded sprang into being. These became her giant sons, who, unsurprisingly, spent much of their time flinging rocks around as their mother had done. However, this pastime was not as purposeful, as it created rockfalls and avalanches and left ungainly outcrops perched in the most unlikely of places. Two of her boys lived opposite each other on slopes divided by a deep valley. When the sun's rays fell on one of them, he was roused to action, which consisted of throwing the largest boulder he could find at his brother on the other side of the valley. The flattened giant would lie there until the sun had moved across the sky and now shone on him. Then he would be revived by its rays, and it would be his turn to act, which involved returning the compliment in exactly the same way. In this manner, the giants' own weapons were used against each other with all the predictability of a megalithic pendulum. After eons of witnessing this, the God of the Sun must have decided to approach Old Mother with a view to creating a child who had some of his father's characteristics and would be able to inspire, rather than terrify, a race as yet to be born – humankind.

Before her last son, Aengus, appeared, Great Mother, Old Woman, maintained the seasons alone. During winter she was a fierce and implacable old woman whose powers weakened as the days lengthened. Then, just before the spring equinox, she would seek out the Green Isle and drink from its well of everlasting youth. During the night whose length equalled day, she would stretch out her own length on the emerald green grass and sleep. In the morning she would awake as a maiden, bringing spring with her on her return home. In her wake would fly flocks of birds, visiting for the warmer months. Flowers bloomed at every step and grass grew lush and green in her footprints. Leaves unfurled like fingers stretching to touch her as she passed, and birds sang greetings from fields and woods. In summer she was a mature woman, her warm breath causing petals to fall, revealing clusters of tiny fruit. As she stretched out her arms, crops grew tall, then bowed towards her with the weight of their ripening. Autumn arrived and she was a plump matron, the grey in her hair heralding the first frosts, her step slow and heavy with the hoard of fruits in her bundled apron. Winter came again and she was a hard, old, blue-lipped woman, arms thin and strong as wind-whipped bare branches, and fierce glances that snapped ice. She was all of these before her last son came. When people followed, soon after, they would remember her mostly in her wintery form.

Some among them, however, honoured her in all her guises, knowing that it was not possible to have plenty from the fair months without life also retreating underground to be replenished by a cold sleep in the darkness. Among these were women who felt the call to devote their lives to the goddess. They had chosen for their sanctuary the island of Jura, for had not the Old Woman of Power left her mark on its landscape visible from around and afar? There, towering above its moors and the sea, were the distinctive tokens of her femininity, bestowers of bounty to all. To this day the people still call these curved mountains, unmistakeable in their shape, 'The Paps of Jura', which means 'Jura's Breasts'. This island also lay near the fearsome whirlpool that Old Woman had created so long ago.

So it was that nine priestesses lived there, like their sisters in devotion far away to the south, on the Island of Avalon. Once called, they lived out their lives on Jura, and when any of them passed on to the Other World, there was always another devotee to take their place. Although no one else lived on the island, they went about their tasks fully veiled – some said it was because one of the meanings of the goddess' many names was 'veiled one'. Others said it was because it showed that their lives were dedicated to a sacred mystery and their veiled forms symbolised that nothing was ever fully revealed. They received no visitors, although when the weather was calm, people used to row over and leave them gifts on the rocks. It was considered a pious act to share what they had to spare with the sister priestesses, and in all other parts of the land, ritual offerings were always made to Old Woman of Power throughout the festivals that marked the seasons. Rarely, a sailor or fisherman in difficulty would be washed up on the island and the women would tend to them out of charity until they were able to leave.

The fame of this island spread far and wide and reached the ears of a prince of Norway, whose king was the most powerful ruler in the region. During a voyage south, Prince Braekan, motivated by curiosity rather than piety, decided to visit the island, even though he knew that it was forbidden to anybody other than the priestesses.

If the holy women knew that he was skulking among the rocks, spying on them, they made no sign, and he continued to observe them from his hiding place. There they were, all nine, drawing water from one of the wells, passing buckets from one to the other in a chain to avoid having to pass over the difficult ground more than was necessary. Braekan was closest to the one who was at the well's edge, when a slight breeze stirred her veil, and for a moment he saw her face. That glimpse was enough for him to fall violently in love with her. Any other purpose in life was consumed by the overwhelming desire to make her his wife.

He rejoined his boat where it had been hiding in the lee of the island's far shore, and his crew was ordered to take him to the mainland with all speed. There, Braekan was granted an audience with the chief druid and asked how a marriage could be arranged. The druid counselled him against any such plan in the strongest possible terms. However, Braeken insisted that there must be some way to get what he wanted. At last the druid revealed that if the prince's boat were able to withstand three incoming tides over the Old Woman's whirlpool, he might thereby have sufficiently challenged The Cailleach's power to make the priestess reconsider her vows. The druid told Braeken that to secure the boat in position over the whirlpool, it would have to be tied with a magical rope to the island of Jura and to the mainland. This rope needed to be made by the plaiting of three strands: one of horsehair, one of wool and one of maidens' hair. Only such a rope would have the power to protect the boat from the whirlpool's fury.

Naturally the local people knew the plan was as foolish as it was disrespectful – but they didn't try to stop him, knowing that he stood no chance of success. They trusted that the goddess knew how to take care of her own. They did not try to stop him but neither would they help him, and all refused to part with any horse hair or wool. When it came to the maidens' hair, they just laughed at him with scorn. So Braeken sailed all the way back to Norway to get what he needed from there, and met with opposition from his father at the advice of the wise men of the court. Nevertheless, the prince prevailed and the rope was made at last. Triumphantly he returned to Scotland ready for his trial against the whirlpool.

Eager though he was, he had to wait. The Old Woman of Power was not going to make it easy for him. First she sent such a strong gale that no boat could set off from the mainland. The fishermen knew better, but time and time again Braeken ordered his own crew to set sail. Time and time again they were blown back. It was a marvel that the ship didn't break up on the rocks but Braeken had to give up eventually because his crew refused to make any more attempts. The gales lasted for three days, but when they died down at last, Braeken did not take the hint. As he tried to set off on the fourth day, a mighty storm arose, the thunderclouds turning the sky as dark as night and a rain of lightning striking all around them. No one could put to sea, and the tempest raged for three days and three nights. When it was over, the prince would still not heed this latest warning. As soon as he could he was ordering his crew to set sail, but before they had hauled anchor, a heavy fog descended, thick as wool, which muffled sound as well as sight. It was impossible to steer a course and the fog lasted for three days. Despite this display of anger from the Old Woman of Power, and the clear warning in its having lasted for nine days, the prince was determined.

He tied the magical rope to an outcrop that had been provided so many millennia before by one of The Cailleach's giant sons. Then he sailed across the whirlpool at low tide and, having first tied the rope around the boat, he swam over to Jura, secured the other end of the rope and then swam back to his boat empty-handed. There he was hauled aboard by his crew and all waited for the incoming tide. The cliffs of the mainland were lined with people waiting to see what would happen. Of the priestesses there was no sign.

With an unseasonal roar, the tide rushed over the whirlpool, which spun furiously. The boat was tossed up and down, but did not turn or get sucked under. When the tide abated, the boat was unharmed but there was no cheering from the onlookers. There, dangling, was the woollen strand. It had broken. All waited for the next high tide. With only two strands holding it, the boat dipped and rolled helplessly but was not sucked under.

When the whirlpool calmed, all could see that she had taken on water, and floating in the sea was the severed horse hair strand. The boat was only being held by the strand of maidens' hair, but the prince persisted.

In came the next tide. Now the whirlpool resembled a great seething cauldron. It heaved relentlessly, hungrily, and the last length of rope broke. Down went the ship to be spat out at last further along the coast, mangled and crushed. The captain found the prince's broken body washed up on the shore. Only he and the prince's dog were there to bury him. The people had not forgiven the affront to their goddess or that they had needed to deplete their winter stores to survive the nine days of her righteous displeasure. You can still see the cave where the prince was buried. In his memory, that dreaded whirlpool was called Corryvreckan, Braeken's cauldron. Nobody tried to intrude on the nine priestesses ever again.

Dagda the Good, Dagda the Generous

Despite being the chief of the gods, Dagda was thought of as being rather rough and ready by some and all too earthy by others. He was a character we may describe in our day as 'a good trencherman', demonstrated in those distant times by his cauldron of generosity, which was always full – unless it was he who had emptied it, as only The Dagda was able to do. Indeed, once, when he had been taken prisoner by his enemies, they foolishly made him eat all of its contents, hoping to have found a means of torture commensurate with his reputation for greed. He took his time, savouring every mouthful, until the suspense almost became a punishment for his would-be tormentors.

They waited a long time to see signs of discomfort or worse, and, just like The Dagda's hunger, they were not to be satisfied. When, at last, it was empty, he painstakingly licked it inside and out and asked whether he could have some more. Otherwise it was perpetually brimming with porridge for all who were hungry. His generosity also stretched to a pair of piglets that, no matter how often they were eaten, always returned to life, thus making it possible to permanently have one roasting on a spit beside the cauldron in readiness for the second course.

But who were these enemies, capable of capturing so powerful a god? The Fomorians were another race with divine powers who inhabited the island of Ireland before The Dagda's tribe of gods arrived. They were the children of the Earth goddess Danu, she whose name is remembered still in places as far apart as Doncaster and the River Danube. Some believed that the Fomorians came from below the ground and some that they came from below the sea. Their powers were those of the elements – the crushing earth, the overwhelming ocean – and they had no horror of destruction and chaos. Many of these giants only had one leg, one arm and one eye, but they still had the strength to keep The Dagda captive, if only for a while, despite his famous weapon of war.

This was a club, so huge and heavy that it needed its own chariot to carry it about. Before the chariot had been built, The Dagda had dragged it along the ground, where it had gouged deep furrows in the Earth. These were used as boundaries marking the borders between provinces and can be seen to this day.

Perhaps this is where another aspect of The Dagda's 'earthy' reputation comes in, as some said that it was not a weapon of war that made these furrows and that 'club' was a polite euphemism for a less detachable and possibly more desirable anatomical feature. His inexhaustible supply of food was a gift from the Earth goddess, with whom he mated to ensure the fertility of the land and the renewal of growth in the spring – hence the club's magical ability in restoring the dead to life with its touch. His consort was The Morrigan, Earth goddess, who was also later revered as a goddess of war and had the power to predict the fate of warriors before the fighting started.

Preparing for a decisive battle between his own race of divine beings and the monstrous Fomorians, The Dagda sought out his Morrigan queen. In a generation's lull in the fighting, there had been so many couplings between his people and the enemy that allegiances were now divided. This mixing, which had produced offspring with split loyalties, would also determine Ireland's fate. The consorts' love making was so intense that as The Morrigan straddled over the land, what gushed from her body became the River Unius. It was then that she used her powers of prophecy to tell The Dagda that their people would win in the last battle against the Fomorians, but would have to pay a great price for victory.

As divinities of fertility, they had many lovers and perhaps one of The Dagda's favourites was Boann. She happened to be married, but that didn't prove to be an obstacle when a combination of passion and divine powers made their liaison both possible and undetectable. Boann's husband, Elcmar, also had divine powers – some say that he was a close relative of The Dagda – and he was chiefly preoccupied with guarding the source of all wisdom, the Well of Knowledge. This was to be found on his land, where nearby lay what is now one of Europe's most important archaeological sites, called New Grange in English. Some say that it was The Dagda's earthly residence but what we do know is that it is a temple to the Earth's journey around the sun. Every winter solstice it welcomes the last shaft of the setting winter sun through its stone passage into the womb of the Earth. There this shaft of light lies buried, whence it is reborn each spring.

The Well of Knowledge was surrounded by a thicket of nine magical hazel trees. In it swam the Salmon of Wisdom, its great silvery body spotted with pale blotches, each one appearing whenever the fish swallowed a hazelnut dropped by one of the overhanging branches. Elcmar looked to this well more closely than he ever looked to his wife, and, apart from himself, only ever allowed his three cup bearers to approach it. Its water to him was sweeter than any wine but for all that it bore the taint of that magical salmon, no special knowledge was revealed to him about was to happen.

The Dagda convinced Elcmar to go on a journey – it would only take a few hours, surely. He then enchanted him so that he would feel neither hunger nor thirst nor tiredness. Neither would he notice the rising and the setting of the sun, changing days into nights, as The Dagda had caused the sun to remain in the sky at its noonday zenith. Thus the unwitting husband would have no sense of time passing. So it was that Elcmar was away for months, believing it to be only for one day. This allowed Boann and The Dagda to enjoy each other undisturbed. However, on her husband's return, Boann discovered that she was pregnant. The timing would have been hard to explain had not The Dagda charmed the sun to remain high in the sky for nine months, convincing all, including the Earth herself, that only a day had passed. Thus their child could grow safely in Boann's womb without her husband finding out who the father was. When he was born, Boann named him Aengus, which means 'my only desire', because of the overriding passion she had felt for his father. Small wonder, then, that this child of passion was destined to become the God of Love.

His father had him safely fostered in another world, and some say that this Other World existed in another time. When it was safe for him to return, The Dagda had already allocated all desirable places to those divinities who had been victorious over their old enemy the Fomorians. These, in turn, were to become sacred to the race of mortals. However, there was nowhere for Aengus to live and he asked if he might stay in New Grange, to which his father agreed. It was then that, like father, like son, he too played a game of time trickery. Aengus used a figure of speech with a double meaning that could be interpreted either as a day and a night or as day and night being representatives of time itself with which to trick his father into letting him stay there forever. In this way The Dagda ceded ownership of New Grange. But what need of a single earthly abode for one artful enough to stop the sun's own journey in the sky? So it was that Dagda the Good, Dagda the Generous, gave his beloved son a place of his own in this world after his being hidden away for so long in another.

BOANN THE THIRSTY

Beloved of the chief of the gods himself, how Boann had thirsted for their embraces, despite her marriage to one who was guardian to Ireland's greatest treasure. Perhaps she also thirsted for the child born of that adulterous union. The baby boy had been taken swiftly to another world before her husband could question the child's paternity. So soon after his birth had she lost him, there had not even been time for her to hold him to her breast.

Now bereft of both lover and child, she was envious of her husband's treasure — the Well of Knowledge, in which swam the Salmon of Wisdom, forever trapped in its watery prison and denied its journey between the rivers and the sea. Why should her husband only allow his cup bearers near this precious well? Why should his wife be denied what his mere servants were permitted? She decided to touch those magical waters herself, but she feared her husband's anger if she were discovered. One night she went down to their cellars, where great barrels of wine and beer and mead were kept. Silently, systematically, she withdrew all the bungs until she was almost ankle deep in the tide of drink that filled the cellar. It was a wonder that the smell of alcohol didn't rouse the whole household, but it must have given them sweet dreams! The following day, the three cup bearers had plenty to contend with without visiting the Well of Knowledge, which is where Boann went instead.

Never having been there before, she could not know how it was protected even in her husband's absence. As she approached, a small wave rose from the surface, questing in her direction. Like a gloved hand, like a blind but keen-scented creature, it followed her every movement whether she tacked forward or backwards. She thought to outwit it by moving in a counterclockwise direction to unwind its spell of protection. Widdershins she approached, in a closing spiral. As she drew nearer, all the force of the well with its watery depths reaching as deep as the roots of the Earth itself burst over its parapet, sweeping Boann away in a great flood. Tossed every which way, first she lost a leg, then an eye, then an arm until she resembled one of the monstrous Fomorians that her lover had defeated in the war over the land of Ireland. At last she reached the sea, where her sweet waters mingled with the salt.

From that day to this has flowed the River Boyne, named after Boann, revered as the most sacred river in Ireland. Her waters touch the sacred site of New Grange, where for a short time in her journey she caresses the home of her lover. That is why the Well of Knowledge can no longer be found, and as for the Salmon of Wisdom, surely he made his escape out to sea? But like all salmon, he eventually made his way upstream and inland once more, finding his way into another story in which he helped King Arthur and his companions to release Mabon, sun child, from his prison of darkness. When the Salmon of Wisdom returned to sweet waters at last, it was to the River Severn ...

THREE JOURNEYS FROM SWEET TO SALT

Lord Plynlimon, genius loci, was the spirit of place of the Cambrian Hills in the centre of Wales. Old as the rocks themselves, he had seldom been seen by mortals. Some said that he was a giant, some that he was so large a giant that it was impossible for a human to see his entire form – his chin being one hill and his cheeks others. Certainly the heights of his domain were so often covered in mist that it could be hard to make out any contours other than those of one's own hand.

Among the oldest in the land, Plynlimon was feeling his age and was concerned for the future of his three daughters. One day he summoned them and explained that when he was no longer with them, they would have their own lands to rule over. That time was nearly upon them, closer than they could have imagined for, during the longest day when the midsummer sun lingered in the heavens, the maiden goddesses were to claim their lands. This was to be done by walking any path of their choosing until they reached the sea. Wherever they had walked on that day would become their sovereign territory as long as their journeys ended when they had reached the land's limit with their feet bathed in salt water – and all before nightfall.

Soon it was Midsummer's Eve and the sisters could barely sleep for excitement. How well they knew their father's country, and over and over they plotted their paths. Fortunately for them, the shortest night of the year was soon over and they could start their journeys, knowing that choice had made them wise to their future.

The eldest, Hafren, who would in time be called Sabrina by the Romans and Severn by the English, had learned how to pace herself. She knew that if she set her stride long and steady, she would be able to keep to it for the entire day and cover a great distance. Not wanting to lose a single moment or a single step, she was up and ready while it was still dark, watching the sky, waiting for the stars to pale. The middle sister, Gwy, or Wye as she was also to be called later, planned her journey according to the most beautiful places she had ever been to – the hidden valleys, lush fields and thick woods where her playmates were deep shadows and sudden swathes of sunlight. As for the youngest, lively Rheidol, she simply couldn't decide which way to go. She changed her mind so often about the direction in which she would set off that if you could have seen her thoughts it would have been like watching the random scramble of wild mountain goats leaping from rock to rock. And how could she go anywhere without her best friend, her cousin Ystwyth, The Agile One? The two were inseparable and some say that they journeyed together, holding hands as they bounded down the mountains towards the sea. When, at last, Rheidol fell asleep, just before dawn, the plans in her head resembled a whirlpool rather than a path.

At dawn, Severn and Wye hugged each other and set off in different directions. Rheidol, like most teenagers, was still fast asleep. So confident was Severn of her plan that she set off in the opposite direction from the sea! North-east she strode before turning south at last and then making a great curve as her journey turned to the south-west, creating the shape of a giant's ear in the landscape. Wye knew she would have plenty of time to meander, to travel in loops and curls, visiting all her favourite places. Her path was shaped like one of the beautiful strands of her crinkly hair. Meanwhile, Rheidol slept on, waking only at midday when the midsummer sun grew too hot for her to stay in bed. Gone were any thoughts or plans, gone too were half her allotted hours of daylight. With the vigour of youth, she sprang along the shortest route to the sea. It was precipitous, even treacherous at times, but her momentum kept her going as she tumbled among the rocks. At times her speed sent her rolling head over heels down steep slopes.

The sea was a field of gold as the setting sun spread its glory over the water. Rheidol tasted salt, but it was the salt of her own sweat. Then came the salt from her tears of frustration and self-reproach. The ocean seemed so far away, how would she reach it before nightfall? At last the land evened out, allowing her to stop stumbling, to ignore that stitch in her side, stabbing with every stride. She watched as the sea turned from gold to copper. Gasping, she ran on. Now the ground beneath her feet had turned to sand, those vast expanses of sand that appear on the west coast of Wales. The tide had turned to meet her. The sun was a crimson sliver on the horizon. It flashed a streak of green, then disappeared as the first salt wavelets licked her ankles.

Severn had turned to the west and Wye had been running due south. Both had been hearing the cries of sea birds for some time. The golden sheet of water seemed to be billowing towards them as the tide surged between the narrow channel that was to divide Wales from England. Then, against the setting sun, Severn saw a silhouette that she recognised. It was her sister, Wye. She splashed towards her through the incoming tide and, delighted, the sisters played together in the waves. Then, suddenly, they felt a great power surging beneath them and found themselves lifted from the water on the back of a huge salmon. Laughing and clutching at each other with glee, they slid from the great slippery back, now spangled silver in moonlight. Again and again the salmon dived and threw them up, and for a few moments the goddesses were embraced by the air as they had been by the elements of land and water. Then the great Salmon of Wisdom, oldest of the old and wisest of the wise, swam on upstream to his hidden pool where he would guard his secrets for another time.

Far away in his domain, Plynlimon, genius loci, spirit of the Cambrian Hills, smiled his wide, slow smile. He was so proud of his daughters: fast, furious and determined Rheidol, beauty-loving Wye, and steady, ambitious Severn. Had any of them looked behind them on their journeys they would have seen water welling up in every footprint they had made. That water now increased, swelled and gushed until their paths became great rivers, sovereign queens of their domains, bringing fertility to the lands they owned. Content to go to his rocky rest at last, giant Plynlimon closed his eyes in sleep beneath the hills. From that day to this, Rheidol and her cousin Ystwyth play together where they empty into the great bay near the town of Aberystwyth. Wye and Severn always remember how they were blessed by the Salmon of Wisdom, who deigned to play with them when their journeys met. Every year they honour his salmon leap by creating a great wave that gathers itself and races upstream. That is when Severina, Goddess of the mighty River Severn, rides the wave on her chariot drawn by dolphins, and today we call this the Severn Bore.

A HAND OF SILVER, A HEART OF STONE

There is no greater need for healers than in a time of war. One of the most skilled was the keeper of the Well of Health, whose magical waters could mend all wounds and cure all sickness. These waters could even halt the journey of the dead as they moved from this life into the Other World.

The well's guardian was Airmid, the most skilled herbalist of the land. It was said that she had combined all her herbal knowledge to make the potion that infused the well water with its magical powers. There was only one condition that it could not cure, and that was to restore life to one whose head had been severed from the body. Airmid was daughter to Dian Caecht, God of Healing, and sister to Miach, the greatest physician that Ireland would ever know. How glad was the Tribe of the Gods to have these healers on their side, restoring health and even life to their fallen comrades as battle raged. They were returning to a land where they had once lived, these descendants of the Great Mother Goddess Danu, whose name they had carried throughout Europe. Now their old home was inhabited by a race of divine monsters over whom they would need to be victorious if they were to reclaim their land. The arena of war, therefore, was one in which each side saw the other as invaders.

The weapons wielded were beyond the reach of mere mortals. Some of the deadliest fighters were born from earlier unions between the monsters and the gods, and it was one of these who wounded King Nuada, leader of the godly race. His life was saved by the Well of Health, but he had lost an arm, and it was the custom then, among both gods and mortals, that no one with an imperfect body could be king. For all that Dian Caecht, with his great powers, had fashioned him a silver hand that moved just as one made from flesh, Nuada was no longer accepted as their ruler. So it was that the kingship was transferred to his nephew, Bres, whose mixed parentage meant that he was a child born of those who had become enemies.

Woefully for the Tribe of the Gods, Bres sided with that of his monstrous ancestry, making his subjects pay tribute to their former enemy. Even the greatest of the gods were treated like slaves; moreover, Bres flouted the first duty of a king – that of hospitality. This endured for years until at last the Tribe of the Gods' poet composed a satire against their king. In the days when reputation was as important as lineage, satirical poetry could cut deeper than any sword. Bres had been given his chance and he had abused it.

The words of the court poet were seized by the winds and spread throughout the land. They sliced through Bres' vain boasts like hail, fell like sweet pollen into hungry mouths, filled ears with murmurs of hope. Even Bres, who thought he could get away with anything, now felt the wind of change.

This was the moment when Miach would show just what his divine art could achieve. With many laying on of hands, many spells and many incantations, he restored Nuada's silver hand to one of flesh and blood, identical to its twin as though it had always been there. Nuada could now regain the kingship, but it was now Miach's name and Miach's deed that filled the voices of the winds as they swept around the land.

As for Dian Caecht, for all that he was the God of Healing, he could not cure himself of the poison that now seeped into every part of him. It made his skin crawl. His stomach twisted and churned until it birthed a bitter foam in his mouth. This poison's name was Envy. He unsheathed his magical sword, of which it was said that only Dian Caecht himself could cure any wound it made. Before him stood his son, who smiled at his father. The sword whispered through the air, slicing at

Miach's head so that a flap of skin was lifted from his brow. Still smiling, Miach stroked it back into place and murmured the words of a spell of mending. Not even a scar showed the passing of that cruel deed. Surely his father had come to see with his own eyes how his powers had grown in the service of their people! Again the sword split the wind and, this time, the blow penetrated through flesh until it met bone. Still smiling, Miach healed himself. His father must be testing him again. But Dian Caecht did not return the smile. It seemed the very power of his sword was being leeched away – this sword whose wounds could not be cured without its owner's say-so. Was even the magic of his weapon to be usurped by this boy? The third blow cut through Miach's skull and exposed his brain. Again that divine touch, those powerful words and no mark left to show what had occurred. But now Miach was no longer smiling, perhaps he was wondering what exactly was occurring, perhaps he was seeing past his own wound and into his father's sickness. The fourth blow struck deep into Miach's brain. The greatest healer of all lay dead at his father's feet. There would be no healer in this world or the next world nor in any of the worlds in between who could cure himself of that death-dealing blow.

So it was that Dian Caecht finally discovered the limits of his son's powers, and the loss of the young man's art for the benefit of divine and mortals alike did not seem too high a price to pay.

It was Airmid who mourned most over her brother's grave. Every day her tears watered that green mound so that its grasses were greener than any in that rain-swept land. A day came when the turfs sprouted green shoots, which turned into plants, herbs and flowers. There were 365 kinds in all, for each day of the year and for each lunar cycle. Together the plants grew in the exact shape of Miach's body. Each kind of plant was found where it could cure any ailment that might afflict that body part. A loving brother had given his sister a gift from beyond the grave – a perfect map of healing. Airmid spread her cloak on the ground and skilfully started to pick those plants, laying them on the cloth in exactly the same shape as they had grown from the earth. So careful was she, so intent, that she did not notice their father creeping up behind her. Dian Caecht could now see that his son's great power reached out beyond his grave, beyond death itself. He waited until his daughter had picked the last of the plants. As she laid it tenderly in place he swooped down and plucked the cloak from the ground and swirled it in the air. The winds came and blew those plants, herbs and flowers throughout the land. From that time to this time, great knowledge was lost, no healer now has the cure for every ailment, and the human race is fated to bear frailty and suffering as part of life.

HORSE GODDESSES

Horse goddesses are remembered in myth and depicted on archaeological remains and in archaeological sites along with ritual practices. Among these divinities are Epona, brought from Gaul via conscripts in the Roman legions, who travelled as far as Northumberland; Macha from Ireland; and Rhiannon from Wales. However strange, distasteful or horrific it may seem to modern readers, there is evidence of ritual sex with mares as part of an initiation ceremony for men about to take leadership of a tribe or region. The mare was then butchered and ritualistically prepared for eating, the ascendant leader even bathing in the broth made from her carcass. This account from Gerald of Wales is not believed by many, however, there are depictions of men having sex with horses on Scandinavian stone carvings, and we know that there was much trading, slaving and settling of Scandinavian people on these islands. It is certain that stories have been shared and co-mingled, and possibly this practice as well. Perhaps the following stories are folk memories of what was once considered divine ritual practices, however difficult it is for our modern sensibilities to imagine or accept.

Were we to be able to set our reactions to one side, we might be able to see the symbolism within these rituals. These practices could be interpreted as the leader consorting with the goddess of the land, manifest in the form of a mare. It is then her sacrifice that nourishes the people and ensures the land's fertility. The stories that remain to us emphasise the pregnancies and births that these horse goddesses go through, and the ordeals that they undergo for the sake of the fertility and wellbeing of the land. Furthermore, there are instances of the children born to these goddesses coinciding with the birth of foals with whom their destinies are linked. Throughout many cultures, this notion of the incoming ruler mating with or being accepted by the all-powerful sovereignty of the Land Goddess was crucial to the survival of crops and harvests and to the renewing of the relationship between peoples and that great force we now call nature. On this island we have carved great equine figures, gleaming white, onto the body of the land herself.

RHIANNON

There was once a lord who, through loyalty, trustworthiness and generosity, had become a great friend of another, one who ruled in the Underworld – that other world where the fairy folk lived. Many times these two worlds would meet, either through encounters between their peoples or at those special times of the year, Beltane, which we now call May Eve, or Samhain, which we now call Halloween. At these festivals the gates of that other world were open and there was mingling beneath and above the fairy hills. The outcomes of any encounters were unpredictable, bringing good fortune to mortals or not, but if any suffered more it was the fairy folk. So it was a blessed time when, with Pwyll as ruler, trust and friendship reigned over all and throughout the worlds.

One day, when he was out riding, his attention was caught by a rounded hill, swelling like the belly of a pregnant woman. His attendant told him that if one of noble blood were to sit there he would either suffer an injury or see a marvel. Drawn to that hill as though his destiny were calling him, Pwyll climbed up and gazed down from its height. At once he saw a huge white horse and riding it a woman dressed in gold. The horse ambled towards the mound, but Pwyll did not recognise the rider and asked one of his attendants to intercept her and ask who she was. An easy enough thing to do, but somehow when his servant reached the place where they would have had to meet, she had ridden far beyond it. He was ordered to fetch the fastest horse in the stable and ride after her, but although that horse galloped flat out, still the magical rider increased the gap between them – although her mount never so much as broke into a trot. Perplexed, Pwyll commanded his companion to try again on the following day, but the same thing happened.

On the third day, Pwyll himself tried to catch up with her but his horse was exhausted before he would admit that he had failed like the rest. Only then did he think of calling out to her:

'Stop! In the name of the man you love the best!'

She reined in the huge white horse and reproached him for not sparing his mount by speaking to her sooner.

Rhiannon explained that she had come from her world to seek him out. She felt that he was the only man for her and had come to find out if he felt the same way. Of course, Pwyll returned her feelings, but was dismayed when he also learned that she was already betrothed to another. Following this encounter, a sequence of tricks was played out by her two suitors to win her for themselves. At last Rhiannon, Goddess of Fertility and Plenty, gave her beloved a magical bag with which to win her back from the man who was not worthy of her. Pwyll was to go to their wedding feast and ask for enough food from their table to fill that bag. The custom was to always fulfil a request granted. Not to do so would be to lose all honour and live a life of shame.

Disguised as a beggar, Pwyll arrived at the feast. His modest request was granted and he proffered the bag, but no matter how much food was stuffed into it, it never got any fuller. How could the bounty of an Earth goddess be exhausted? No mortal would ever have enough food to fulfil that task, because that bag, created by the goddess herself, was the mouth of the whole world, limitless in its capacity.

Rhiannon's unwelcome fiancé had to admit defeat and was advised that the only way the bag could be declared full was if a nobleman stamped down the contents with his own feet. This the host did, but as soon as he stood on the food, Pwyll's soldiers, who had been hiding, rushed in and drew the sides of the bag up around him and tied them together. Then they set about beating him until he was only released on condition that he promised never to pursue vengeance. However, when he took this oath his mouth spoke the words from a lying heart. As the path of happiness stretched before the new couple, beside them stalked a terrible and secret revenge.

Time passed and Pwyll's nobles were concerned that his marriage had not been blessed by an heir. How could he assure them that sovereignty was truly his, sanctioned by the Goddess of the Land, when there was no new life to prove and bless it? Perhaps he was married to the wrong woman; after all Rhiannon wasn't one of them, she had appeared rather mysteriously after all, and perhaps she should be put aside and another wife found? Pwyll resisted these insinuations and after a third year Rhiannon gave birth to a son.

Her women watched as she rested after the birth, but after midnight, they too fell into a deep sleep and when they awoke the baby had disappeared. They were so frightened at what might be their punishment for neglecting their duties that they hatched up a plan to protect themselves. A bitch had just produced a litter, so they killed some of her puppies and smeared Rhiannon with their blood. When she awoke and asked them where the baby was, she herself was accused of having murdered and eaten him. Truly there must have been some evil afoot for such a lie to be believed, but believed it was and the falsehood was spread throughout the land.

Again their ruler was asked to put aside his wife, but still he maintained his faith in her. When she realised that she could not persuade her servants to tell the truth, Rhiannon decided to stay at court and accept her punishment, innocent though she knew herself to be. How would this sickness in the land be expiated if she was not there to see an end to it? She was compelled to sit by a mounting bock and to tell passers-by what she had been accused of and then to carry them on her back as though she were a horse.

Meanwhile, in another part of the country lived a man who was famous for his stables. He owned some of the best horses in the land. His favourite mare would always foal on May Eve, but then, that same night, the foal would simply disappear and nobody knew what became of it. In that same year, Teyrnon decided that this could go on no longer and resolved to keep watch when his mare was due to give birth again. He had her brought into the stable and at twilight a large sturdy foal was born. As Teyrnon approached it, he heard a scraping sound outside that set his teeth on edge and made his skin crawl. There, reaching through the door, was a huge claw. It was this that had scraped down the outside wall, searching for an opening. The claw was followed by a great scaly hand attached to a monstrous arm. Then the claw searched out the newborn and hooked into his mane. As the animal was being dragged towards the door, Teyrnon drew his sword and hacked off the arm at the elbow. There was a scream so terrible that he nearly lost his reason as well as his hearing, but still the brave man pursued the thief into the darkness. However, it was too dark for him to see the assailant and he rushed back to the stable as he realised that the door had been left open and the foal was unprotected.

Dark though it was, something glimmered on the threshold. It was a garment of gold cloth. Inside it was a baby boy. Teyrnon took the child to his wife, who had none of her own and wanted to keep him. She told her husband that she would make her servants lie about her having gone through a pregnancy. From the first, that child was bigger, stronger, quicker than any of his own age. He couldn't be kept away from the horses, always playing at being one of the grooms, until the woman suggested that he be given the foal that had been saved on the night he was found. In her mind, the saving of the foal and the finding of the child were inextricably bound. Teyrnon agreed but suggested that she should be the one to give it to him as as she had been the one to name the boy, according to custom.

In time news reached them of what had befallen Rhiannon at Pwyll's court. This gave the couple much to think about, and as the boy grew, Teyrnon saw how much he resembled Pwyll, for whom he had worked in the past. The couple realised the identity of the child they were keeping and agreed to return him to his rightful home to end Rhiannon's punishment. Great was the joy at court when the three of them appeared. The couple refused any gifts or recompense and the righteousness of their good deed became an act of healing for all the land. The heir they had restored to his parents grew to become one of the greatest heroes that Wales had ever known. Under his rule, child of the Horse Goddess Rhiannon as he was, peace and plenty ruled with him.

Faster than Horses

There was a widower whose lands were extensive but at a distance from everyone else. There he lived and farmed with his motherless sons. Maybe he was a good farmer, maybe he kept the balance between what his family and the wild places needed – he never knew the reason for his visitor, but there she was.

Silently, one twilight, the woman stood on his threshold. He hadn't heard her approaching, he hadn't seen which direction she came from, she was suddenly just there. All he knew about her was that she was not of his world. He was too astonished to be frightened as she stared at him with huge dark eyes. Without knowing, he had risen to his feet and there they stood, two worlds meeting, no time passing until, full of wonder, he stepped aside and that movement was her invitation to enter. No words passed between them as he watched her move about the place, knowing where everything was, how to set things right, how to transform a house into a home. When his sons came in, lantern lit from the deepening dark, it was as though their mother had never left them.

Together they lived as a family as though that was how they had always been – except that now everything they turned a hand to prospered and increased. Their crops were the heaviest in the land, the ewes all produced twin lambs, the cows, twin calves and the mares, twin foals. The woman rarely spoke, so when she did she was listened to. Her voice seemed to come from far away; it had an echo to it, like a voice thrown into a well or speech in a cave.

'Macha, my name is. Macha, the plain that bears the most fertile land. The plain with the gentle curves where horses can race the wind that blows so freely.'

Time passed without notice but there came a day when there was to be a great fair nearby. It seemed that everyone of any importance from the whole of Ulster would be there. The place would be heaving with stalls and entertainments from blacksmiths to bardic contests and chariot races. Even the king himself would be there. Macha showed no inclination to attend but her husband was eager to be off – he would never have seen such an exciting gathering. As he was about to leave, there she was on the threshold again with that dark look of hers. Her hands moved to her belly, swelling now with new life. She said but one thing to him before she stepped aside to let him pass, 'Have a guard on your tongue. Don't let it gallop away with you.'

He left, still listening to the echo of her words. Perhaps they went too deep for him to recall them, for he was soon caught up in the excitement, his head swirling with the new wonders of the day, that stretched into others, each with its different delights. Then the last day of the fair was upon them with the most thrilling of all the events – the horse races. Of course, the king's horses won all the heats. At the last of the chariot races, the king's steward stated the obvious by saying that none were faster than the king's horses. It was ill luck that Macha's husband was within earshot, 'My wife is faster than any of the king's horses.'

This outrageous statement could not go unchallenged. The steward brought him before the king, where he was made to repeat his rash words. Whether to demonstrate how ridiculous the claim, or whether out of angered pride, the king ordered his wife to be brought to the race course and to race against his horses.

Soldiers arrived at the distant farmhouse and told Macha of the king's command. Heavily pregnant, she could have gone into labour at any moment. She told the men that she would attend the king after she had given birth, but they insisted that if she did not come, her husband would be put to death. At that she ran to the assembly. When she arrived, her labour pains had started. She asked the king and all his retinue to show compassion and wait until her labour was over – had not every person there been born through their mother's birth pains after all? However, the king was adamant and would not soften his command.

Macha's anger surpassed his. She looked with scorn at his retinue, not one of whom having dared to intercede on her behalf. Her voice carried over the multitude, her words whipping across their ears like jockey's blows on horse's flanks.

'Any harm to me will be as nothing to the harm that will befall all of you for generation after generation.'

It was only then that the king listened, asking what her name was.

'My name, Macha, and my children will be remembered in this place forever.'

Then, despite being in labour, she raced against the king's chariot. Running side by side, their speed ate up the distance of the course, but she was holding back. Nobody was cheering for the king's horses. The crowd had been silenced by the woman's unnatural speed and strength, by the creeping certainty that they were watching something more than they could understand.

Towards the finishing line Macha sprinted forward, reaching it first. There on that other threshold that now marked the line between cruelty and compassion, respect and insult, her twins tumbled from her body to the ground. There they lay in the path of the oncoming chariot. How had it come to this? From careless words, to obdurate challenge, to a course hurtling towards all that was wrong and unnatural in the killing of newborn babies? The nightmare continued as the charioteer struggled to slow the horses, failed to slow the horses. Some could not bear to look any more, some did not want to look but were unable to turn their heads away. It was those who saw the horses rear up between the shafts, rising like a wave that parted as the beasts, still on their hind legs, their hocks almost gouging the ground, turned aside from those helpless children, bursting the frame of the chariot to spare them injury.

All those men of Ulster who were present heard Macha deliver her curse against them and their descendants for nine generations to follow. They too would endure the same labour pains, but these would last for five days whenever they were at war and needed to be at their strongest. But they, being mortals would suffer weakness like mortals, and not endure like a goddess.

So it was that both Macha's prophecy and curse came to pass. That place is known to this day by a name that means 'The Plain of the Twins'. Throughout hundreds of years, the men of Ulster were unable to fight for five days at a time, which severely affected their fortunes in war. Macha never returned to her careless husband. He and their half-brothers raised the twins between them. There was never fence nor wall that they couldn't clear in one jump, they would run faster than any river in spate and, hand in hand, outrun the wind itself on their mother's plain.

4

Tales of Love and Passion

Dream Lover

I will find out where she has gone,
And kiss her lips and take her hands;
And walk among long dappled grass,
And pluck till time and times are done
The silver apples of the moon,
The golden apples of the sun.

William Butler Yeats, 'The Song of Aengus'

Deep beneath the ground in her father's palace, with her multitude of sisters, lived a swan maiden, able to take on human or bird form at will. Her father was royalty among the fairy folk – those who had once been gods and goddesses in their own right. But already their world was changing and some, like this fairy prince, had become forerunners of the fate that would overtake all gods and goddesses. They would eventually be confined to the wild and secret places, or to those where daylight could not reach them beneath the Earth. In the eyes of our world, their divine powers would wane to mere caprice and trickery, feared rather than revered by we mortals.

This the swan maiden knew, Goddess of Prophecy and Dreams as she was. She was named after the fruit of the yew, a tree that was holy to the druids. These mortal priests practised their art in sacred yew groves, striving to keep to the old ways and beliefs and thereby achieving the gift of prophecy for themselves. Thus they too became messengers between this and other worlds. The glowing lamps of the yew berries against the green-black of the foliage would tempt them to dare their deadly poison, bringing on the visions sent to them from another world, while risking that they would leave this one forever. In honour of this practice, the swan maiden was called Yew Berry, and her full name, 'Castle of Yew Berries', referred to those groves sacred to the druids, where lesser mortals would not dare to penetrate.

Some say that she preferred her swan form as it allowed her to travel in those elements – air and water – that were denied her in her goddess shape. Otherwise she moved upon the surface of the Earth, or felt too keenly its confinement in her father's palace below the ground. Some say that is why she only chose her human form at Samhain, the festival that we now call Halloween, when the gates between the worlds are open. Others say that this was the time when she transformed herself, year and year about, alternating between her swan and maiden form for a year at a time.

Yew Berry had the power to send dreams to mortals and gods alike, and when she slept, her own dreams were prophecies. It was through her own dreaming that she foresaw the passing of all the goddesses and gods into the world where her father ruled. One night, in her maidenly form, she dreamed of her future lover. There was no one in any of the worlds more worthy of her love and to receive his love would be the greatest of blessings, as her dream lover was no less than the God of Love himself.

Aengus was the son of Dagda the Good, the sun god. His passion for Boann led him to halt the sun in the sky for nine months so that Aengus could be conceived and safely brought to term without Boann's husband knowing. Aengus' name had several meanings or titles – Mac Og, for one, meant 'young' because, once the boy had been safely fostered in another world, his mother wanted her miraculous pregnancy to be remembered, 'Let him be called "Young" because eternally youthful will be the child conceived in the morning and born between that same day and evening …', crowed the Goddess Boann.

Aengus was the protector of lovers, whether it was lovers fleeing from authority, spouses or jealousy. He flouted convention and ensured that true lovers found a way to be united, even if their liaisons were to end in tears. Passion was paramount and had to be fulfilled, whatever the consequences.

Unsurprisingly, Aengus frequented the Land of Eternal Youth, that other world where mortals went when they had died. There they were given the choice to remain forever young if they were willing to pay the price of giving up their memories. Those who preferred to keep the hardships of old age and illness, rather than surrender their memories, were pitied by Aengus the Youthful, who would never know infirmity or ageing. He would visit them as they sat around a fire, trying to ease the chill in their old bones. Pitying the discomfort of age, he would cheer them by telling tales of goddesses and heroes, magic and marvels.

In those distant times, birds were rarely seen on Earth, reserved as they were by the gods to take messages back and forth between the worlds. Birds were created by Aengus' kisses, and he always had four flying around his head. One of these, Redstart, followed the god's example in pitying the weakness of the mortals on Earth. When she was sent with divine messages, she noticed how people suffered because they had not yet received the gift of fire. Aengus interceded for her with his sun god father, chief of the gods, to allow fire to also be shared with the living. Since then, we too have always shared stories around the fire. In its glow our capacity to love is rekindled and its heat reflects our passion.

Deeply asleep in his own sacred home at New Grange, Aengus was dreaming. In his dream he saw a maiden playing a harp. Slowly, she moved towards him, her fingers never straying from the strings, never missing a note. It was as though his whole body became that instrument. Her nails, lustrous and shapely as shells, were playing on his heart strings, plucking every sinew. His being thrummed with love, he knew he would never find a more perfect lover, he knew he would never want to. Far away in her father's fairy world, Yew Berry was conjuring Aengus' dream, shaping it, sending it luminous and clear, moving closer to him so that he could see the golden flecks in the irises of her eyes, the flare of each perfect nostril like the curve of bird's wings. She had chosen her dream lover and he was now in love with a dream.

Love-haunted by night, he sleepwalked through the days without eating, longing only for the time when he could return to his bed, sleep, and dream of his love again. Always she came close; always when, knowing that she was more than a mere dream, he rose to touch her, just as skin was about to greet skin, she faded away. Her music remained for a few moments after the vision had gone, and his ears could even snatch those lingering notes when the pain of her leaving had woken him. After months of not eating, he was too feeble to leave his bed. He did not complain as, in his weakened state, it was easier to pass into sleep where she waited for him in his dreaming. After a year, a physician attended him and knew instantly what was wrong. He listened to Aengus' description of his dream, consulted with his mother and asked Boann to search the whole of Ireland for the goddess her son had fallen in love with. Perhaps Yew Berry was in her swan form, because although Boann searched for the whole year, still she could not be found. By now Aengus had been pining for the love of his dreams for two years.

When Boann's search had failed, the physician counselled that Aengus' father be involved in saving his son. However, The Dagda did not see how he could help or how he could find one who had eluded them for over a year. But was he not the chief of the gods? Did this not still include the fairy folk in their forts beneath the turf, inside their mounds and hills? Surely this vision must come from among them. Surely, Bodh, King of the Munster fairies, being the wisest among all of the tribes, would know who she was or where to find her. And why wouldn't Bodh be only too glad to help, being Aengus' uncle?

The Dagda's request was well received at Bodh's court. The messengers were welcomed with a great feast and after the eating, the dancing and the music, it was time for the storytelling. On this occasion, King Bodh waved away his court storyteller.

'Wouldn't I be the best one to know the harm that can come of unrequited love? If there is anything I can do to bring true lovers together and avert another tragedy such as happened to that poor fool who courted my own daughter, surely I would, and why wouldn't I do as much for my own nephew?'

His guests listened to a tale that Bodh's people remembered only too well, for hadn't they lived through it themselves?

'Not so long ago, a harper came courting my only unmarried daughter. I didn't take to him for all his skill. Oh, but couldn't the sweetness of his playing bring out the blossom on the apple boughs in the midst of winter or the fish leaping out of the river to get nearer to his music? He could even play quite different tunes with his two hands at the same time. Haven't I seen him myself conjuring bright sunshine and summer breezes in one half of the sky with one hand, while gathering storm clouds and thunder with the other?

'As I said, I didn't take to him myself, for all his art, but I kept my own counsel until I knew what my daughter thought about the man. Too much sorrow has been caused by jealous fathers. Great was my happiness when I saw she was of the same mind and there would be none of this nonsense of slipping away in the night or escaping by some trickery. His suit was refused, but he refused to leave, still seeking to charm his way into my daughter's affections with his incessant playing, until she would go about with her ears stuffed with lambs' wool. His music did not call to her the way this maiden's music echoes in my nephew's heart.

'To protect my daughter I brought down a mist over the whole hill, so that he would not find the entrance to our fort, or better still, would get lost among the hills and wander away. But he remained, forever playing, and from time to time we would hear the strains of his music drifting through the mist, so we knew that he was still about the place. Without his or our knowing, that constant playing had roused a dragon that lived beneath my own fort. The first we knew was a trembling in the ground, then a shaking so violent that it twisted all the rocks of the mountain. When the monster burst through the ground, my mist was burned away in a moment, and we could all clearly see what happened next. The beast made for the harper and swallowed him down in one gulp. Then it sighed deeply, setting fire to everything for as far as the eye could see. Then it turned and disappeared back down to its lair.

'Whether it swallowed the man because it was a torment to have its sleep disturbed or whether it loved the music and wanted to keep the harper with it forever, I didn't ask, and there was my own place going up in flames around me. It used all my power to summon enough rain to put out that mighty fire, and so a great lake was formed in my mountains that was never there before, and is here to this day, and don't my people still call it the "Lake of the Dragon's Mouth". Nothing can save that fool of a harper now and what a greater shame it would be if love requited is not united. If I can turn the tale of my nephew's dream to the good, I will do it, for all it may take another year of searching.'

Bodh was as good as his word, but it did take him a whole year before he was able to send a message that he had finally found the maiden from Aengus' dream – and wouldn't you know it – she had been found at the Lake of the Dragon's Mouth!

When this news reached Aengus, hope cured where all else had failed, and he was well enough to ride his chariot to meet his uncle in that place. There, from the shore, they saw one hundred and fifty maidens bathing in the lake, sisters all, but as alike as twins. Splashing and playing two by two, sister was joined to sister, a silver chain linking each pair.

'How will you know your own among them?' asked Bodh.

Seventy-five pairs linked by a silver chain, or not quite, because one was alone, and the only one with a chain of gold. Aengus recognised his dream lover instantly, despite the tears that blurred his sight now that his long waiting of three years was over.

But it was not to be so simple. Finding was not keeping, and Bodh was wary of kindling any cause for conflict among his fairy kin. Yew Berry's father would have to be approached with care, so Bodh suggested that the mortal king and queen of that place ask for her hand on Aengus' behalf. In the days when the gods were recognised and revered, Queen Maeve and King Ailill were honoured that this divine party was asking for their help and they hastened to comply. It was they who sent the request to Yew Berry's father. Time passed into autumn and still they received no reply. At last they discovered that, alas, their message had not been well received. Furthermore, Yew Berry's father refused to attend their court or speak to them about his daughter other than to say that Aengus' suit was denied. This filled Bodh with foreboding, but it filled The Dagda with rage. Was he not the chief of the gods? Who did the fairy prince think he was dealing with to dismiss his cause so casually? He gave the order for the fairy court to be attacked and for the father to be brought before him as a prisoner.

When this had happened, the fairy prince explained that his daughter could never marry because she was under a great enchantment that even he could not undo as she herself had created it. This was to spend one year in the form of a swan and one in the shape of a human maiden. The Dagda demanded to know which form she had taken at the present time, and heard that she had shape-shifted into her swan form. They all hastened to the Lake of the Dragon's Mouth and there, on this occasion, they saw one hundred and fifty swans swimming, paired by silver chains all but for one, who swam alone with a golden chain about her neck.

Now that Aengus knew her name, he called it and the swan left the others and came to him. All looked on and saw how two swans were before them on the shore, for, as they watched, Angus too transformed himself into a swan. Yew Berry's golden chain extended itself to loop around his neck, then the great birds paddled their feet on the surface of the water and rose into the air. Joined together by more than their chain of gold, they flew three times around the lake, singing all the while. Then they flew across Ireland towards Aengus' palace at New Grange, where they were to live together in happiness. As they flew, they sang so sweetly that all who heard them fell into a deep sleep for three days and nights. We may be sure that all those who slept that long sleep also dreamed of their dream lovers.

Yew Berry's father was overjoyed that his daughter had been accepted for who she was and the shape that she herself had chosen. True love did not alter when it alteration found, to quote a later bard, and true love did not hesitate to join her in her own form. The fairy palace was restored and peace was made between its prince, the mortal king and queen and The Dagda, chief of the gods. That was a rare time when gods and goddesses, the fairy folk and mortals could meet, each from their own but other world, to do good deeds together.

***

Near to where this author lives, a remote farm had been hiding a Roman secret. Valued in its own time, it became a treasure in ours. The mosaic depicts the story of legendary characters, lovers so famous that they have been remembered in visual art, poetry and opera. Gods and goddesses had decreed that one of these was to become the founder of Rome. His descendant, in turn, was also driven by destiny. A wanderer like his great-great grandfather, his landing is commemorated by the Brutus Stone in Totnes, Devon. Sailing up the River Dart, Brutus landed to engage in victorious battle with the giants who, in those distant days, inhabited this island. When they had been conquered, Brutus gave his name to the land of Britain.

Beneath the field, his great-great grandfather's story lay sleeping in the dark, dreaming the same dream over and over again, captured forever in its thousands of tesserae. Perhaps the goddesses and gods who had created that story were also asleep in this land that no longer revered them. Perhaps it was merely an accident of nature, not Jupiter, that unleashed the fatal lightning that struck dead the farmhand rushing to protect the hay from the oncoming storm. His daughter, eldest of six, told me how she saw the discovery of that mosaic unfold. The burial of a sheep had revealed what had been a prized part of a Roman villa. Creeping through the hole in the hedge that adjoined the find and the farmworker's cottage, she would see how more of its images were being revealed as the dig progressed. Almost undamaged by trauma or time, it was rolled up like a giant carpet and can now be seen laid out in all its splendour in Somerset's County Museum in Taunton.

PUPPETS OF THE GODS

Cesser d'aimer ou d'etre aimable, c'est un mort insupportable –
Cesser de vivre ce n'est rien

(Ceasing to love or to be loveable is an unendurable death,
Ceasing to live is nothing)

Voltaire

How can mere mortals, helplessly shaken by their passions like a rag doll in the hands of an angry child, know that their feelings are not of their own making, but inflicted upon them in the service of the gods? So it was with Dido and Aeneas, who at last found hope in each other after they had lost everything they had cared for.

Dido's husband, king of a country we now call Lebanon, had been murdered by her own brother. This knowledge came to Dido in a dream, and when her brother seized power she believed it and knew that her life too was in danger.

She managed to escape by boat with a few loyal servants and came at last as a refugee to a part of coastal North Africa we now call Tunisia. There she sought help from the local king and was welcomed as a guest. However, her host soon wanted to marry her and Dido refused him. Despite explaining that she had taken an oath to never remarry, the king still pressed his suit. Knowing that she could no longer remain in his court, Dido begged for some land to be given to her for her own. Ungracious to the last, her rescuer refused. Then, publicly, Dido begged for a piece of land that could be encompassed by a single ox hide. To have refused such a small thing would have brought ridicule, so her request was granted.

Of course, the largest available hide was chosen, but then something unexpected happened. Starting on the inside and working her way outwards, Dido instructed her most skilled servant to cut the hide into the thinnest possible strip, rather like when we try to peel a whole apple without the peel breaking. Everyone watched, bemused, as this was done. At last the hide lay on the ground looking like a vast severed tree trunk with all the rings of its many years showing where the skin had been cut through. Then the ingeniousness of the plan was revealed when her servants carried it some way along the coast. Having judged a sufficient distance, they gradually unrolled what had become a leather skein of string and stretched it round a piece of land as far as it would go. The space it encompassed was sizeable and it was hers. That is where Dido began to build her city, Carthage, whose ruins you can see today near Tunis.

Far away, on the coast of what was to become Turkey, Troy was burning. One of its vanquished heroes, Aeneas, was escaping, carrying his old father on his back and dragging his son by the hand. In the melee he became separated from his wife. He had wanted to stay and fight but, in a vision, he had been ordered to leave by the spirit of his slain commander. Now that his wife was lost he turned back into the flames to search for her, but she was already dead. Then her ghost appeared and told him to flee and to found a new city in the west. With nothing left to lose, he managed to assemble a fleet and sail westwards. But Aeneas had more than mortal enemies – Juno, queen of the gods on Mount Olympus, hated him because he was a Trojan. She had wreaked her revenge on all Trojans ever since one of them had chosen Venus, Goddess of Love, as being the most beautiful of all the goddesses instead of choosing her. Juno also knew that Aeneas was destined to found a city that would be at war with a people who were under her protection. Most important of his unwitting offences against her, however, was that Aeneas was Venus' son, and Juno would never forgive her for having been declared the most beautiful among the divine.

Whatever Aeneas' destiny, Juno could nevertheless make him suffer. She persuaded the God of the Winds to create a storm so that the fleet would become separated and destroyed. This plan was working until Neptune, God of the Sea, took exception to her meddling in his realm. He calmed the ocean just in time for Aeneas' vessel and some of his companion's boats to be saved. They came ashore at Dido's new city. As a refugee herself, and one with manners befitting her royal status, she welcomed the fugitive warmly.

This was Venus' chance to thwart Juno and ensure the safety of her son. She appeared to Aeneas, dressed unusually in the garb of a huntress, and counselled him to make love to Dido. As her consort, under her protection lay his safety. But honourable Aeneas, pious Aeneas, knew that the destiny his wife's ghost had spoken of could only have been some divine message. He knew that his fate had been determined by some greater god. Founding a new city would change the face of the world and compensate for the one he had lost. Who was he to refuse his part in the divine plan? Who was he to refuse his mother also, and she too a goddess?

Venus had a rather different approach to Juno in getting what she wanted: her gifts were wrapped in the silky veils of desire and her weapons were naked passion. As was the custom, Dido gave a feast for her honoured guest and as was also the custom, the hostess was given gifts. The manner of their presentation was almost as important as the gifts themselves, the practice being imbued with great ritual significance. Venus sent her son Cupid, bringer of desire, to the banquet, disguised as Aeneas' own son. Nobody recognised him as being anyone other than the most precious being in Aeneas' life – the hero who had lost his country and by now all other members of his family. The little boy solemnly staggered up the aisle, his arms heavy with gifts. By the time he had reached his rescuer, childless Queen Dido, everyone's heart had melted. Dido gently took her presents and placed them on the table without looking at them. Her empty arms reached for the child and lifted him onto her lap. How she cuddled him, fed him titbits from her own plate, encouraged his childish prattle. Before the feast was over, her vow to widowhood was forgotten. Dido was ready for love.

Soon after, having arranged a hunting party to entertain her guest, Dido and Aeneas became separated from their companions during a storm. Seeking refuge in a cave, their sudden and overwhelming passion ensured that nobody else would have been welcome. Venus had stalked her quarry well, brought it to earth, and left it dead to all other commitments. On returning to the court, Aeneas gave his lover his sword as a token of his loyalty.

It was as though they were the first lovers who had ever existed and the only ones who ever would, so great was their happiness.

Oblivious in their bubble of delight, neither noticed that time was passing. But destiny was growing impatient – Aeneas was visited in a dream by Mercury, messenger of the gods. Mercury reminded the sleeping hero of his duty to found a city in the west. When he awoke he knew that he must leave even if his departure were to break his lover's heart. Dido pleaded with him to stay but he would not.

As his fleet put to sea, Dido ordered a great fire to be piled up in the palace courtyard. The servants thought it was for burning Aeneas' remaining possessions, and indeed Dido was flinging onto the flames anything of his that could be found. When all traces of him had turned to ash, she climbed the palace walls. There was something of his, however, that had not been thrown onto the fire. From her belt hung Aeneas' sword. Dido looked at his retreating ship for one last time, then plunged the sword into her body and leaped into the flames below. She suffered the ritual threefold death of a sacrificial victim, dying of a broken heart, at the point of a sword and by fire. Perhaps Juno took some fleeting satisfaction in Dido's last words turning to vengeful fury as she cursed Aeneas' future by wishing war between his new nation and hers. From his ship, Aeneas saw the distant smoke of Dido's funeral pyre. He didn't know what was burning, only that it was a bad omen. It was fulfilled many years later in the long Punic wars between Rome and Carthage.

SPRING LOVE

Aengus, God of Love, Youth and Summer, was sleeping away the winter on the Green Isle of Eternal Youth. In his divine dreams he was able to see what was happening throughout his beloved lands, and especially likely to attract his notice was a desirable woman. So it was that he dreamed of Bridie, Goddess of Spring, who was being kept captive by his mother, The Cailleach, Old Woman of Power. In his dream his mother appeared in her fiercest aspect, her spellbinding powers keeping the land locked in bitter winter, just as she kept her servants bent on fulfilling her commands.

There she sat on her snowy throne, Ben Nevis, highest mountain in the land. With a gaze as clear as the icicles that fringed her robe, she kept watch on the season and whatever her servants got up to. Harsh as the north wind were her commands, and all knew what had befallen her handmaiden Ness, who had failed in her duty. This was to tend a well high up on Ben Nevis, which had to be covered every sunset and uncovered at every dawn. One evening Ness had reached the well later than usual and it had overflowed in a violent flood, threatening to sweep her away. Terrified, Ness had rushed down the mountainside, trying to escape, when the commotion had attracted Old Woman of Power's icy glare. Within a moment she knew what had happened and called out, 'I see you running there! As you run now, may you run forever!'

The poor woman was turned into the River Ness, whose flow was so great that it created a huge lake. When this threatened to flood the land, Old Woman reached down and pinched a passage to the sea, creating Scotland's largest loch. As for Ness, she is fated to keep on running, so to this day, her river continues to flow into the loch. Many places remember her story, including the town of Inverness.

In his dream, Aengus could see another woman who was being harshly treated. Woman or goddess? Aengus could not imagine that one so lovely could be a mere mortal. But if she were a goddess why was she unable to resist her servitude? Day after day she was washing a fleece, trying to get it clean for her mistress, the Old Woman of Power. Whether she washed it in the sea, under a waterfall, or beat it on the stones of every loch or river in the land, it never looked any cleaner. Day after day her mistress told her to try again and Aengus realised that this beautiful creature was none other than a form of Bridie, Goddess of Spring. His mother, the Goddess of Winter, was keeping her busy, distracted from her true purpose so that she could not blossom into the spring that would defeat winter. Even before he realised this, Aengus was falling in love as fast as a torrent rushes down a mountainy slope, as deep as the deepest lake. When he awoke he thought about how he could help to free her so that her own power could blossom, and, being a god, it wasn't hard for him to come up with a plan.

The next night, when Bridie was asleep tired out from her useless labours, it was her turn to receive a dream that was not just an ordinary dream as it was a vision that Aengus was sending her. In it she saw herself washing that cursed fleece yet again. Did it even follow her into her dreams? But as she watched, an old man appeared and whispered in her ear. Despite the rushing of the waterfall, she could hear him clearly.

'I have a gift for you, but first you should know that the fleece you are washing will never be clean because it has never been dirty. It is from one of the wild sheep of the mountain, not one of the pale sheep from The Old Woman's fold. You are trying to turn dark wool that has always been brown into wool that will never be white. When you tell her that you have discovered her trickery, her power will be weakened. It will weaken even more when you show her these.'

Then the old man laid a bunch of snowdrops in her lap and disappeared.

Bridie awoke, smiling, feeling happy for the first time she could remember. That smile was like the first ray of spring sunshine after a long winter. As she stood up, something fell to the ground. It was a bunch of snowdrops. Then she went to The Cailleach to tell her that she would work for her no longer trying to turn a brown fleece into a white one. At this, Old Woman's sharp features seemed to soften, angles melting into curves.

'You have never given me wages for my pains, yet I have a gift for you.'

When Bridie laid the snowdrops before her, Old Woman's icy gaze blurred and tears ran down her face. Then the young goddess, no longer a servant, turned away and went to the western shore. Before long she saw galloping towards her a great white horse, its hooves skimming the white horses that were the crests of the waves. On it rode Aengus, her dream lover from the Green Isle of Eternal Youth. When he reached the shore, he scooped Bridie up before him and together they rode to do battle with The Cailleach, Old Woman of Power. In every hoof print, water welled as the snow melted. The wind of their passage was soft rather than bitter, and left a sweet sound as all the icicles started to drip their different notes. But this was what Old Woman had been waiting for. As soon as she had been given those snowdrops, harbingers of winter's end, she knew that the fight was on, the fight against her own son. She knew too that each battle would make her weaker and him stronger. However, with Bridie's help he would be fit to take over the precious burden of ensuring that the seasons would each take their turn in reigning over her land. How tired she was, how she longed to rest until autumn's storms heralded her return. But, first the fighting.

She summoned her eight servant hags, Frost, Ice, Hail, Thunder, Snow, North Wind, Blizzard and Cold. From all directions they swooped down on Bridie and Aengus and drove them back, westwards over the sea. Again Aengus and Bridie returned, again they were driven back. To and fro, from land to sea and sea to land and back again raged the war. Aengus was fighting for the sake of his beloved Spring, but it was only the month of February when the weather can be as wintry as ever. Being God of Summer, he chose to borrow three days from August, his hottest month. With these at his command it grew suddenly warmer and the hags of winter began to tire. They were giving ground. Each time the lovers returned, their journey towards the heart of the country was longer. At last, with a furious shriek and one last bitter blast, the hags retreated northwards, and the land was left to Aengus and Bridie. That night they slept in each other's arms, and if they dreamed, it was only of each other. Summer had returned at last, but could never have done so without first being in love with Spring.

From that time, February has always been Bridie's month. She is forgiving about the trick her mother-in-law played on her with the fleece. Instead, she has a special fondness for flocks of sheep, protecting the ewes and making sure that they have enough milk for their lambs. Imbolc is her festival in early February, the feast that celebrates 'the lactation of the ewes' when, in the north, the first snowdrops can be seen. In later times, when Goddess Bridie became Saint Bridget, her association with flocks and herds increased, and it was said that a snowdrop appeared for every drop that she milked. As for Old Woman of Power, she thought that any trick of stealing days from other months that her son could do, she could do also. That is why, at the end of summer, she borrows three days from February to use during the last days of August. Then it suddenly blows cold, a warning of what is to come as the summer slips into autumn. That is why, from that day to this day, in Scotland, there are always three unexpectedly warm days in February, and three unexpectedly cold days in August, and in this way the balance of the seasons is restored.

SONG, POETRY AND LOVE

There were three men came out of the west,
their fortunes for to try
And these three men made a solemn vow
John Barleycorn must die
They've plowed, they've sown, they've harrowed him in
Threw clods upon his head
And these three men made a solemn vow
John Barleycorn was dead
They've let him lie for a very long time,
'Til the rains from heaven did fall
And little Sir John sprung up his head and so amazed them all

They've let him stand 'til midsummer's day 'til he
looked both pale and wan
And little Sir John's grown a long, long beard
And so become a man
They've hired men with their scythes so sharp
To cut him off at the knee
They've rolled him and tied him by the way,
Serving him most barbarously

Steve Winwood, Traffic,
'John Barleycorn Must Die', adapted from the tradition

The mixture of song, poetry and love would be hard for any to resist and if your enjoyment of poetry and singing were sustained by the caresses of true love, why would you want to? And if such incomparable bliss had once been enjoyed, how would you live without it? But, true to the complex shape of myth, whose tendrils of consequences grow in all directions and whose vagaries of fate may appear from any, I seem to be starting this story in the middle ...

Anyone would have thought that Daphnis, singer and goatherd, was born for love. However, he appeared to be more the object of such devotion rather than returning it as unstintingly as his lovers would have wished. His early life was mysterious in that, though born of divine parentage, he himself was mortal. His father, Mercury, messenger of the gods, had left a nymph pregnant after their liaison. Not wanting to rear him herself, she abandoned her son under a laurel tree. There he was found and suckled by a nanny goat and, soon after, adopted by the shepherds to whose flock she belonged. They named the baby 'Daphnis', which means 'laurel', after the tree where he was found. Perhaps in this naming, there was also a premonition of the competitions that the boy would win as a young man, at which victors would be crowned with laurel leaves. Reared in the peaceful and lovely countryside, his heritage could be seen in his divine singing voice, his masterful compositions and his having been the first to discover the genre of pastoral poetry.

Only to hear him was to fall in love, and although mortal, in some places he was elevated to godly status where shrines were dedicated to him as a divinity of the seasons and nature's renewal. Despite numerous dalliances, some of which ended tragically for his lovers, or would-be lovers, his affections endured for the nymph Pimpleia. She was named after the birthplace of Orpheus, the greatest musician that the world had ever known. Some said that she was a manifestation of Thalia, daughter of Jupiter and muse of Comedy, whose name meant flourishing or blossoming. Some said that it was she who developed the art of pastoral poetry and gifted it to her lover. Whichever versions were true, it seemed to be a relationship made in Heaven that blossomed and flourished on Earth, until the day Pimpleia was abducted by pirates.

After the raid, surviving witnesses told Daphnis what had happened, but nobody could say where the pirates were sailing to. Daphnis must have felt that this was some kind of divine punishment for neglecting all those other lovers who had so adored him. Now all he could sing were laments as he prepared to search the world for his beloved. Singing for his passage on any boat that would take him, so beautiful were his sad songs that the crews put up with the lack of variety and mingled the salt of their own sorrows with that of Neptune's element. How strange it was for Daphnis, divinity of all the moods and seasons of the Earth, to be imprisoned by a boat on this watery world.

At last, after many years of fruitless searching, they arrived at a place with a strange and disturbing custom. It was said that any young man who embarked would be captured and made to compete with the king himself in a reaping contest. This was strange enough, but most concerningly, those who lost would be decapitated and their remains ploughed into the ground where they would nourish the next season of crops. Moreover, King Lityerses always won. It did not take long for Daphnis to discover that Lityerses was the son of Ceres, Goddess of Crops and Harvests. The reaping contest was a ceremony held in her honour and the countless young men who had been cut down were symbols of the many stalks of corn that her bounty had bestowed. Daphnis, with his deep connection to nature and his pastoral upbringing, understood that this was an ancient practice of human sacrifice to propitiate the goddess against future famines. He also knew that he was a herder of flocks, not a farmer.

As the crew was persuading him not to disembark, Daphnis heard something that left him unable to believe his ears. It was singing – a voice he recognised – a song he had composed. There on the quayside was Pimpleia, whom the pirates had sold as a slave to Lityerses. With a cry she recognised, he leaped towards her but just as they were about to fall into each other's arms, he was seized by the king's guard, delighted that here was a stranger and the contest could happen without one of their own being sacrificed.

Perhaps Pimpleia truly was a manifestation of Thalia. If so, it may have been she who prayed to her half-brother, Hercules, to save her beloved. When Daphnis, suitably anointed and robed for the ceremony, was presented before the king, nobody could tell that Hercules himself had taken on his likeness. He was presented with his sickle (which had been secretly blunted by the king) and the contest began. Nobody and nothing could equal the power of Hercules, who reaped his entire field before the king had finished a single row. Hercules' sickle swept one last time, and that was to remove the king's head. The lovers were reunited and cherished each other to the end of their days.

United after Death

The course of true love never did run smooth …

William Shakespeare

Baile was so irresistible that men and women alike fell for him. However, he disappointed them all except for Aillil, a young woman whose jealous father was related to Manannàn mac Lir, the God of the Sea. Knowing that her father would never allow them to meet, the lovers did so in secret and it was during one of these trysts that tragedy struck. However, this was no unlucky twist of fate, but a malicious plan to prevent them from being together no matter what the cost.

Aillil could not risk being away from home for long, so it was Baile who had to undertake the long journey. Before it ended, he needed to rest his horses and release them from the chariot to drink and graze. No sooner had he done so than he noticed an ominous sight moving towards him faster than a storm wave, faster than the stoop of a sea eagle. Baile was filled with fear, but whatever it was came on so quickly that he knew he could not escape even with his horses. The terrifying being hovered near him, and, his teeth chattering with fear, Baile forced himself to ask who he was and what his mission. There was no way for the young man to tell that he was speaking to Manannàn mac Lir himself, shape-shifted into a monstrous form to intercept him with the message that his lover had been murdered. There was no way, either, for Baile to know that this was a wicked lie. When he heard that terrible news, Baile dropped dead with shock.

Manannàn mac Lir flew back to accomplish the rest of his plan, which was to tell Aillil that her lover was now dead. As soon as she heard this, she too died from the shock. Where Aillil lay, an apple tree began to grow, reaching its branches in supplication to the sky. The branches stretched and formed themselves into the shape of the woman from whose body it grew, so sculpted that anyone who had known her would have recognised her easily. At the same time, a yew tree was growing from where Baile had fallen. Its crown formed into a perfect likeness of him.

In time, when the disappearance of the lovers had been noticed and their images recognised in the yew and apple trees, their story was fitted together piece by piece between their households. Then their trees were cut down and their timber cut into wooden tablets. On these were carved love poems, including one that had been written to commemorate their story.

Every Samhain, the holy festival when the gates between this world and the Other World are open and which we now call Halloween, King Cormac would hold a great feast. The high point of the festivities was when the bards would recite poetry. On this occasion, the king's chief druid carried in the tablets made of apple and yew wood. As soon as he spoke the first words from the poem describing the lover's fate, the wood began to writhe in his hands. From the tablets emerged the curved forms of roots and branches, reaching not upwards but towards each other. More and more twigs and branches appeared, seeking, finding, entwining until it would have been impossible to separate them. All watched silently. Aillinn's and Baile's love story had not been heard, but it had been witnessed. Then the vision disappeared like ash on the wind. So that their story would not be forgotten, King Cormac gave the order for an avenue of trees to be planted outside his court. On one side grew yews and the other, apples. Perhaps these too arched towards each other, entwining wherever they touched.

5

Tales of War and Conflict

The First Sacrifice

Before Time was new, there was on Earth a perfect being, one of righteousness and love. Sun God sent him an instruction through his messenger, the raven. When Mithra heard this message he was appalled because it was telling him to kill the most beautiful creature on Earth. Mithra struggled with himself; he was not able to bring himself to do what he must do, which was to follow Sun God's command. How could the source of all goodness and life itself be telling him to kill White Bull? Why kill a creature of power and beauty, one whose immense strength was never measured against the weak? Why kill White Bull, who would nuzzle from Mithra's hand and who loved and trusted him?

Mithra could not pretend that he hadn't heard that command, nor that he hadn't understood or remembered it. As his knife sliced into the bull's neck, he turned away from the sight of his blood. But even through his closed eyelids he could see a great light that forced him to look round to see what it could be. Now there was no blood or body of the animal to be seen. White Bull had become the moon and was rising into the sky. A wind came and tore away Mithra's cloak, which rose up and beyond the moon, becoming the firmament in which planets shone and stars twinkled. Then to each heavenly body came their own dance. At different speeds they wheeled and criss-crossed the sky, encountering partners at times, disappearing over the horizon edge of Mithra's cloak, but always to return sooner or later, because Time too had been born and all now danced to Time's measure.

Only White Bull's tail and genitals had remained on the ground. From his tail, corn and grapes sprouted and spread across the Earth. Sacred seed seeped from his genitals. Mithra collected this in a bowl and from then on all the animals were shaped with a mixture in which this seed had been blended. Sun God was so pleased that he alighted on Earth in his chariot. There he feasted for the first time with his beloved son Mithra, on meat after the first killing of an animal and on wine and bread after White Bull's gifts. Together they rode over the ocean, across the sky and onward to the furthest reaches of creation.

But the light of the moon, rising from the ground, had awoken creatures of darkness who now crept out of the soil to steal the gifts that White Bull had left. Snake was seeking to lick any spilt blood and scorpion to seize the sacred seed. Then began the conflict between light and dark, good and bad. From that time to this time all people have had that conflict mirrored in their lives, teetering between or choosing to take action towards good or evil.

THE DEATH OF CONNLA

Cu Chulainn, son of the God of Light, though still a boy, already showed promise of becoming the greatest fighter Ireland would ever know. For his training he was sent as a young man to Scathach in Scotland, she who taught all the best warriors. Scathach knew that here was the student she had been waiting for – the one to whom she would bestow a unique gift. This was a weapon the like of which had never been seen before, and with it came the secret of how to use it. It had been made from the skeleton of a sea monster that had in its turn been vanquished by some other beast from the deep. Its bones had been washed up on some distant eastern shore, where it had been fashioned into a spear-like weapon that always proved fatal. It penetrated through the belly and then burst into many separate barbs beyond the entry wound, disembowelling its victim. Then it could only be retrieved by cutting open the corpse and disentangling it from its many points of contact. It had made its way westward, passing from the hand of great warrior to great warrior until at last it had reached the mighty Scathach in Scotland. Some say that she had given it to her daughter, Aife, and that it was she who gave it to Cu Chulainn when she fell in love with him. However it was Scathach who revealed how to use it. Perhaps because of its watery origin, it always had to be deployed near water with the end of its haft steadied between the wielder's toes.

The time came when there was nothing left to teach the hero and when he said his farewells as he prepared to return to Ireland, he too left a gift for Aife. This was their son, Connla, quickening in her belly. Cu Chulainn gave the baby's mother a gold ring and instructed her to give it to the child when he was big enough to wear it on his thumb, and then to send him to

Ireland. The boy was also to be instructed never to turn aside for anyone, never to deign to reveal his identity and never to refuse combat.

Before eight years had passed, all happened as the hero had decreed.

Cu Chulainn's warrior host noticed a strange craft shining offshore in the rays of the setting sun. It was a boat made of bronze and a child was rowing it with oars of gold. How the slanting light played on that shining figure, how fast the child rowed, the golden oars spinning beside him so that it seemed as though he was flanked by chariot wheels of light. Deep inside Cu Chulainn and his oldest companions, something stirred, shimmered, as though it were reaching out towards that radiant sight, light calling to light. But before it could dawn into a memory shared, the boy stilled the oars, and the moment was lost. He reached down to piles of small stones in the bottom of the boat. These he fitted into his sling shot and fired them into the air with such skill that for each pebble, he brought down a bird from the sky. Then it seemed that he added magic to skill, for breathing on each bird it was as though he returned life to each one, casting them back into the air where they flew as though nothing had happened to them. Then he distorted his face until such a strange sound emerged from him that he was able to alter his voice to a pitch that made all those birds drop insensible into the boat once more. Again he was able to bring them all back to life.

On seeing this, one of the greatest of the warriors was horrified and wondered what harm the boy's kindred, fighters from an unknown people, would be able to do to them. Surely if a mere child could do this, what feats could his tribe visit upon them that they would have no defence against? He suggested that someone should go to talk to the stranger and instead of welcoming him to land, which was the custom, to find a way of preventing that from happening. The most eloquent and diplomatic among them was sent to the shore to speak to the boy, but he arrived just too late. The child had already landed and so was told to advance no further and to identify himself. Then there was a stand-off as the child refused to reveal who he was, and, moreover, insisted on obeying another of his instructions, which was to stand aside for nobody. Continuing on his way inland, he passed his interceptor, who begged him to return, but the child would not. Then he was promised a welcome from all the heroes of the land if he would cease shaming them by distaining to tell them who he was. His skills were praised, but at the same time he was warned not to incite the anger of the best warriors in the land. This was the opportunity for the boy to obey his last instruction – not to turn away from any fight. It was as though he welcomed the threat and replied with a taunt, 'Ask your host whether they will come against me singly or all together. It will be all the same to me. So it is for you to turn back, not me. If you had your strength a hundred fold you would not be able to stop me.'

As neither eloquence nor diplomacy had prevailed, someone sterner was sent to deal with the boy. This was Conall Cernach, a fearsome warrior who wore the heads of his enemies hanging from his belt and never slept without at least one of these trophies beneath him. But the child spoke to him dismissively while fitting a stone to his slingshot. The missile knocked Conall head over heels. Before he had managed to struggle upright, the boy had mockingly stolen the strap from the man's shield, 'You don't seem to know how to use your shield anyway, so you won't be missing this,' said that cheeky boy, adding insult to injury as he dangled the torn leather in his enemy's face.

Conall returned to the onlookers and suggested that someone else try to deal with the child, but by now nobody was willing, except for Cu Chulainn, already flushed with anger, who started towards him. However, his wife Emer was with him and in a flash of intuition realised who the child was. She begged her husband not to fight his own son. Cu Chulainn, already past mere irritation, was also beyond reasoning as he felt his battle fury stirring within him. He lashed Emer with his tongue, 'Do I need to listen to a woman telling me who I should or shouldn't fight? Is it your place to meddle with such things? This is the kind of glory for kings. Already I seek to feel that boy's blood spurting from his wounds on my skin. Whoever, whatever, is on that shore, I will fight for the glory of our land.'

Cu Chulainn approached the boy and warned him that he would die if he did not tell him who he was. The boy took the threat as a challenge and declared that he would fight. He flew at the man with his sword and sliced off all his hair and beard. Then Cu Chullainn challenged him to wrestle, but the boy said that he would not be able to reach as far as the man's belt. So he stood on two stone pillars and threw his adversary down three times without even shifting his position. So great was his power that his feet had sunk into the very stones up to his ankles. Then they wrestled in the water, where the boy ducked his adversary twice. However, rather than letting himself be brought low for a third time as had happened on land, now that they were in the water, Cu Chullainn was able to use his dreaded spear that spared no foe. The weapon was thrown and disembowelled the boy. As he felt his wound, he cried out that Scathach had not taught him how to use such a weapon and it was only for that reason that he was now meeting his death. On hearing this, Cu Chulainn recognised his son at last and, gathering him in his arms, he lifted him from the water and carried him, dying, to the warrior host.

Connla's last words were to tell them that had he lived he would have conquered lands for them that would have stretched as far as Rome. He then asked to be taken to each one of them to say farewell and to embrace them, and the last one of these was his own father. Grief at his death spread throughout the land. The mourning feasts lasted for three days, for which all the calves in Ulster were slaughtered, and a stone was raised for him where he was buried.

THE BATTLE WITH THE GIRDLE OF THE WORLD

If you were to go to Gosforth Church in the north of England you would see an old cross, some eleven hundred years old or so, and you might wonder whether you weren't also in the Norse of England. There, carved into the most Christian of symbols, is one from a pagan Viking myth. A scene from that story featuring their Thunder God, Thor, is also to be found depicted inside the church. While King Alfred drove off or converted the pagans from the south and west, he was compelled to treaty with the Vikings who remained in the north. Some gradually accepted the new religion, some clung to the old. In Gosforth you can see how history and place once entwined these belief systems and where, even today, the Almighty Sky Shaker is represented alongside the Almighty Father.

Thor was always at his happiest when on some adventure using his incomparable strength to combat some adversary worthy of his divine powers. Sky God, Thunder God, Storm Rouser, Sky Shaker – he who made the Earth tremble – whenever Thor pitted his strength aided by his trusty hammer, he was invincible, or thought he was.

There was one monster he had not yet conquered and that omission cried out to Thor for remedy. If he were capable of blushing he would have done so when he remembered a previous encounter with this creature. But Thor was incapable of feeling humiliation, it was too subtle for him. However, his skin turned as red as his beard with rage when he remembered how Loki, trickster god, had once fooled him during that unfortunate incident when Thor had seemed incapable of lifting a cat. Loki had transformed the appearance of the great World Serpent into that of a domestic feline, which in front of fellow gods, Thor had been unable to pick up. It was only when Loki was convulsed with laughter and no longer had the focus to sustain the illusion that Thor saw his arms were around the belly of the Great Worm itself. This gargantuan beast was longer than the world is wide, girdling it beneath the oceans with its tail locked in its mouth. There was only one way to get his own back on Loki, and that was to kill the World Serpent – no matter if the world then flew apart without its monstrous belt holding it together!

Thor would need help in this enterprise as the monster lived at the bottom of the ocean and the services of a vessel and a seaman would be required. What was tricky was that no ordinary sailor would suffice – it had to be one with the strength of a giant to be able to steer and steady the boat during the combat, so only a genuine giant would do. Thor's relationship with the giant race was not a good one, as no encounter had ended without a massive fight, so he decided to adopt a disguise before approaching Hymir, a giant known for his fishing skills. Thor then changed the appearance of his body into that of a young stripling and in his enthusiasm almost forgot about his rather distinctive beard. In his haste he shaved himself with his war axe and the mottled result aided his disguise in that he looked like one of those youths who insist on shaving before there is sufficient growth to trouble a razor.

Even among giants, the law of hospitality is respected, so Hymir invited this unexpected visitor to stay the night. Before dawn he was ready to put his boat to sea and was rather surprised that his guest was also making ready to join him, even asking if he could have a go at rowing the boat. Hymir didn't want to be hampered by someone who wouldn't have the strength to do much rowing and who would get so cold that he would soon be begging for the fishing trip to be cut short, and said so.

Thor was so furious at being taken for a weakling that he quite forgot that he was in disguise and was about to hit Hymir with his hammer, but then thought better of it as he wanted to save his strength for the World Serpent. Swallowing the insult, he still asked to come, and out of politeness to a guest, the giant reluctantly agreed. When he was asked what bait would be available, Hymir said that the youth would have to provide his own, hoping that this would put him off. Thor looked around to see what he could help himself to and noticed his host's herd of oxen. While Hymir was busying himself with the boat, Thor chopped off the largest ox's head and stowed it at the bottom of the boat under a sail. It was so heavy that it slowed their progress, not to mention that Thor had failed to disguise his immense weight along with his appearance, so they reached the fishing waters later than the giant had hoped. However, Thor still asked to keep rowing until, at last, Hymir was reluctant to go further for fear of the World Serpent whose waters they were entering.

Still Thor insisted on going further out from shore until even he was satisfied, and baited his rod with the ox head. It was a morsel too delicious for the serpent to resist, but he soon realised that he had swallowed more than the meat as the hook stuck in his gullet. The creature's struggles were so violent that he nearly dragged Thor out of the boat, skinning the god's wrists on the gunwale as he did so. So enraged was Thor at this that he tapped into the fullness of his divine strength and succeeded in hauling the monster up against the side of the boat. Hymir was horrified as it glared at them from just under the surface and blew a fountain of poison at them. Thor could only think of how much he would like that head as a trophy to put on the wall of the feasting hall in Asgard.

Then two things happened at once. Thor threw his hammer at the World Serpent's head just as the terrified Hymir seized his knife and chopped through Thor's fishing rod. The serpent sank back to his watery home, where he remains to this day and where, hopefully, he can still hold his tail in his mouth despite the presence of Thor's hook. The god was so furious with Hymir that he punched him overboard with one blow. Although that was enough to send the giant to the bottom of the ocean, he wouldn't have retrieved Thor's hammer, as, when wielded in battle, it always returned to the god's hand.

MONSTER MENAGERIE

The new order was being established when gods and goddesses warred against the divine race of Titans, who so far had ruled unchallenged. Now there was a bid for power from this new race of divinities. Jupiter, mightiest of the gods, had risen up against his own father, Cronus, who had swallowed most of his children, fearing that they would depose him. Had he not brought this fate upon himself by attacking his own father, Uranus? How right he was to fear his own children, and so, before they could move against him, he managed to swallow most of them. However, Jupiter, the most powerful, had escaped. Knowing that he couldn't win this fight alone, he sought help from a Titan whose realm was the ocean. Metis, famed for her wisdom and cunning, created a salty potion that made Cronus vomit up his children. Then, just as their father had feared, the siblings united to destroy him.

Metis was not only wise, but desirable, and Jupiter pursued her. Changeable as the watery element in which she had been born, Metis shape-shifted into animal form to elude him. But Jupiter was a shape-shifter too and pursued her in any form that would be likely to capture her. If she became a dolphin he became a whale. If she became a doe, he became a wolf. If she became a lioness, he became a lion. So it was that he coupled with her and she became pregnant.

Maybe it was a rumour, maybe it was malicious gossip or maybe it was a prophecy that told Jupiter that his children would become more powerful than himself. Like son, like father, like father, like son, Jupiter, warned by his family history, was not going to allow that to happen. He was determined to be one step ahead of the pattern. So he visited Metis and without difficulty persuaded her to play the shape-shifting game once more. He explained that, just to be fair, this time round, he would only take on a form that could be chased by hers. So it was that when he became a thicket of berries, she became a bear, when he became a dove, she became a tree snake; when he became a drop of honey, she, pregnant and unable to resist, became a fly. Where was her wisdom and cunning then? As soon as she had transformed and landed in the honey, Jupiter, instantly regained his true form and swallowed her whole, just as his father had done with his siblings.

Although Metis was no more, elusive as a fly, her pregnancy survived, having found its way from Jupiter's mouth to further inside his head. As the foetus grew, so did his headaches, until at last, unable to bear the pain any longer, he ordered the Smith God, Hephaestus, to chop into his head with an axe to obtain some relief. When this happened, Metis' daughter emerged, fully grown and armour clad. No newborn's whimper for her – her first sound was a war cry. Minerva, Goddess of War and Wisdom, protectress of heroes, claimed her place among the new race of divinities.

However, Jupiter's wife Juno, Goddess of Marriage and Childbirth, was outraged. Was it not enough that she had to put up with his philandering ways? How dare he also usurp her maternal role? Juno decided that she could manage perfectly well without her husband and did one better by going it alone. Being a goddess, she could make herself pregnant without having to swallow someone else's pregnancy first, and resorted to parthenogenesis. The time came for her creation to be born, but unfortunately she gave birth to the biggest monster the world had ever known. Typhon, with a face only his mother could love, terrified all the other divinities when he swooped over their palaces on Mount Olympus, his enormous wings blackening the sky, plunging day into night.

Before Typhon was confined to an abyss, he flew off to meet his fellow monsters who, in those turbulent times, teemed throughout the elements. Surely he was king among them all, and Echidna welcomed him as her consort. Unique among the monstrous sorority, she boasted the head and torso of a woman with everything below consisting of a giant snake. Their coupling was so joyous that it caused avalanches and earthquakes, and cracks appeared in all the Olympian architecture. From this union was born another unique contribution to the monster menagerie: the Chimaera. Formed with the body of a lion, from which protruded the body of a fire-breathing goat, the Chimaera was finished off with a tail that ended in a serpent's head. It ranged about the countryside, burning crops and devouring livestock, which is where we shall leave it for now as we have been without a mortal hero for too long.

Bellerophon was reputed to have two fathers – one a king, and the other Neptune, God of the Sea. This was not unprecedented as royal females were sometimes visited by a divinity, perhaps with the express purpose of bringing another hero into the world of mortals. As a young man, Bellerophon had accidentally killed another and, sent into exile for his punishment, became the guest of a neighbouring king.

There his hostess took a fancy to him, but when her advances were rejected, she complained to her husband that their guest had tried to violate her. Not daring to break the laws of hospitality, but wanting the youth to be punished for this crime, Bellerophon was sent off to yet another nearby court, that of his host's father-in-law. The pretext for sending him there was the delivery of a precious object, one that nobody else could be entrusted with. Little did Bellerophon know that he was carrying his own death warrant – that small bundle contained not treasure but clay tablets. These were inscribed with a message requesting that their bearer be put to death for having tried to rape the wife of one who had given him sanctuary, the avenger to be her father.

By this time, Bellerophon had unwittingly developed quite a reputation for himself, that of a murderer and a sexual offender. But perhaps there is protection for the innocent after all. This king was so pleased to receive a guest that the feasting started immediately and lasted for nine days. To his credit, Bellerophon had tried to impress upon him the importance of what he carried, but was told that there would be plenty of time for that later. When at last the message was read, there was of course the complication that the intended victim was a guest and the law of hospitality still applied. This quandary was solved by sending the young man off to despatch a monster – none other than the Chimaera. The monster had proved impossible to kill and everyone who had attempted to slay it had instead met with their own death. In this way, this latest host could keep his hands clean and exact revenge while the accused attempted something useful.

Like most heroes, Bellerophon rushed off willingly with no idea of how to succeed where all others had failed. His journey took him past a temple dedicated to Minerva in which he stopped off to pray for her help in his quest. Noticing that it was getting dark, he decided to spend the night in the temple, and it was there that he fell asleep. Maybe because he had first shown due respect to the goddess, or maybe because she was also the protectress of heroes, Minerva sent him a dream. It seemed to Bellerophon that he was gazing through a golden mesh that dazzled his eyes, until he was able to look through it to where an even greater brightness awaited his sight. There stood a brilliant white stallion with wings as large as his body. As he watched, those wings unfurled and beat the air until their wind swirled him away into the past, and he was watching an earlier moment in this magical creature's story.

Another hero, Perseus, was holding up a polished shield towards a monstrous head, wreathed with writhing snakes. The shield had become a mirror in which Perseus could see Medusa's reflection. Had he looked at her directly he would have been turned to stone, the fate of all who looked upon her countenance. Without danger to himself, he could use her reflection in his shield to aim her a death blow and strike off her head without looking at her directly. With one pass of his sword, the hideous head fell to the ground. Her petrifying eyes were closed and the snakes lay still. No blood fell, instead a blur of white rose up and great pale wings unfolded, bearing the neighing stallion aloft. Pegasus, the winged horse, was born. Stern Minerva smiled to see this most exquisite of hybrids, and smiled as the hero she had helped presented her with Medusa's head to be worn forever on her breastplate.

Then the picture in Bellerophon's dream receded, grew distant and dwindled until his eyes, now refocused, could see that the golden mesh was a bridle. When he awoke, that bridle lay beside him.

Not long after, Bellerophon found Pegasus drinking from a well almost as though he had been waiting for him. Until now, nobody had ever been able to ride him, but Bellerophon had the goddess' gift of the golden bridle. As soon as it touched the stallion he became gentle and suffered the young man to mount. Then the great wings bore him above the forest and from that height it was easy for the rider to see where the Chimaera was from the smoke trail marking its path of destruction. Descending, Bellerophon was still unable to get near it until he thought of a plan of attack that would keep him and his mount safe, but would prove fatal to the monster. It was a daring plan, using the creature's own weapon against itself.

The hero acquired a lance, which he tipped with lead. He knew that he might have only one chance. Brave Pegasus bore down on the monster from above while the infernal goat's head belched balls of flame towards them. Flying as close as he dared, Bellerophon threw his lead-tipped weapon down the goat's throat. The lead melted and suffocated it. Trickling through the goat's body, it burned its way into the lion's belly and finished off that part of the monster, too. Bellerophon was now a hero and after this act of bravery and cunning became a career hero, accomplishing many great feats, and always with Minerva supporting his cause.

Would that his own head had been struck off in one of his quests because an unconquerable enemy, Pride, had entered it and taken root. Bellerophon, urging noble Pegasus to fly higher and higher, took a notion to visit celestial Olympus. Surely such an illustrious hero would be welcomed by the divine hosts as a guest? Uninvited, he flew nearer and nearer. Outraged at his hubris, Jupiter, already known for his way with flies, sent a horsefly to sting Pegasus under his tail. The stallion reared and his rider fell off. Down, down Bellerophon fell. Blinded and crushed by his fall, he was doomed to crawl over the Earth until his death, which was all too long in coming. As for beautiful Pegasus, Jupiter did not want him to suffer because of his master's folly, and took pity on him. He reached out, grabbed him by a fetlock and flung him even further into the heavens. There he remains, his brightness undimmed. We see him in the night sky, forever flying, as the constellation Pegasus.

WAYLAND SMITH

Wayland, the stout-hearted hero endured troubles,
had sorrow and longing as his companions,
Cruelty was cold as winter – woe found him
Once restraints were laid on him …

Adapted from 'Deor's Lament'

Freya, Goddess of Love and Fertility, was Odin's favourite lover. Although he also had many others, he was furiously jealous when he discovered that Freya had spent a night with each of the four dwarves who, in return, had made her the most beautiful and magical necklace ever created. The dwarves were such extraordinary craftsmen that much of what they made was imbued with magic. Odin had no sympathy for any need that Freya may have had for this exceptional piece of custom-made jewellery. He ensured that it was confiscated, and Freya ensured that it was returned. To kiss and make up, Freya suggested Odin should share her spoils of war. This offer was for his daughters, the Valkyries, to choose who would die in battle and who would survive. Of the fallen, the Valkyries would choose who had been brave enough to be taken to the warriors' heaven, Valhalla, where they would be hosted by Odin himself, All Father and God of War.

When they were not influencing the outcome of various skirmishes, protecting their favoured heroes, dooming others who did not please them, or combing through the corpses on the battlefield to see who was worthy of their father's hospitality in the afterlife, the Valkyries were taking their lovers among both mortals and gods. Three chose to be the lovers of three brothers. One of these was Wayland, the Smith God, whose armour the sisters wore as they swooped over the battlefields. So skilful was he with his hammer that the goddesses teased Thunder God, Thor about Wayland being his natural son. Whether that was true or not, he had been born to a mortal queen, but had shown such talent that he had spent many years studying his craft with the dwarves. So magnificent was his work that his forge always had a host of Valkyries around it, vying with each other for the finest breastplates or helmets or jewellery to be shown off at the banquets that took place between the fighting bouts.

Small wonder that a Valkyrie had claimed Wayland as her own, and the other two were glad to choose his brothers to have Wayland's skill near at hand. But passion can be as fickle as the fortunes of war, and the Valkyries came to tire of these lovers.

The brothers then chose a life in the wilderness, wandering north among the forests and lakes. After many months of roaming, they came across a particular lake in which many beautiful women were swimming. Their pale bodies shone more brightly than the light on the water, but, nevertheless, among all that shimmering beauty, the men were able to discern which of the maidens pleased them the most. All along the pebbled shore lay their garments – great swan wings and downy skins – for these were a group of swan maidens who delighted in swimming naked in their human form. Just like any flock, they left the water with one accord, and ran to where they had left their wings. The brothers knew that if they could seize their swan feathers, the maidens would have to remain in their human form – but how would they choose the right ones among the great drift of wings that whitened the shore line? All was splashing and laughter and even hissing as the maidens dressed themselves in feathers once more, a turmoil of bare legs and wings, flowing hair and arching necks. But there among the melee, three maidens were walking towards them, carrying their swan wings and downy swan skins. They were the three that the brothers had longed for.

Each swan maiden placed her wings and skin before her chosen man and stood upon it – each one before the man who would have chosen her. Everyone knew what that gesture meant. Each would be with her man when she chose. Each would come and go as she pleased, in any form that she chose. The brothers were full of joy. Their days of wandering were over. Home, hearth and love awaited them. They made their homes by the lake for the sake of the swan maidens. Lovers, sisters and brothers were content. Wayland was a wanderer no longer. His new-found happiness led him to rediscover the passion for his craft, and so he built himself a forge. Just as he as kindled its first fire, so did the spark of inspiration urge him into new creativity. No more would he make weapons or armour, now that all was peaceful within and around him, he would only use his skill in the service of beauty.

So it was that Wayland began to make exquisite jewellery whose quality rivalled even that of his teachers, the dwarves, who had taught him all they knew so very long ago. The clearing where they lived became his treasure house where the tree branches were festooned with his work. There necklaces and torques, bracelets and slender twigs encircled by rings, sparkled in the sun. On and on he worked, contented with his new life and with doing what he did best.

One day the King of the North Lands was riding along that lake, having become separated from his hunting party. Searching for signs of them, his eyes ranged along the treeline, brilliant in its autumn colour. At first he did not notice the gleams of gold among the glowing yellow of the alder leaves. Then, as he drew closer he could not explain those flashes seeming to accompany the breezes that stirred the leaves, and he allowed curiosity to draw him closer. The clearing was empty. The swan maidens had flown off to visit their sisters, and the brothers had formed their own hunting party to lay in supplies for the approaching winter.

All around the king, Wayland's work flashed and tinkled and the king wanted it. Greed made him want to fill his saddlebags, stuff his shirt. But he had been king for long enough not to be an impulsive man. He was alone and unarmed. A brief search revealed dwellings and a forge – whoever made these treasures would return, and the king planned to send his soldiers to capture both the wealth and the man who had made it. It was so hard to resist taking more than one item. Among so many just one would not be missed, would raise no suspicions, but what to choose? There, near the tip of an upturned twig, was a ring so delicate in its twisted gold that you might say that it was woven from maiden's hair. Wayland had made it as a gift for his beloved swan maiden, a thank you present for returning to him as she always did. The king marvelled at how it caught the light and thought how his daughter would love that ring. He seized it and galloped off to court, his hunting party forgotten now that he had found a more precious quarry.

Wayland returned with one of his brothers, the youngest lingering behind to make a birch sled to drag their kill. Despite the fading light the smith noticed that one of his pieces was missing. It was not to be found, even on the ground beneath that branch, on the ground where he could now see hoof prints. But just as understanding came, the ambush was sprung. The king's soldiers surrounded the brothers with chains at the ready. How humiliating for Wayland that he should be captured in this way, trussed up with chains not of his own making. Blindfolded, he had to listen to metal upon metal as the soldiers shoved his work into bags, or hoped to get away with stealing something of what their master had not yet counted.

Then followed a bumpy ride – different sounds and voices, more rough handling, blindfolds being torn away and dazed sight taking in a banqueting hall – the cruel gaze of its king and, behind him, two smirking princes. It was not hard to know which of the prisoners was the smith, with his huge shoulders and forearms as thick as most men's thighs. The other brother was dragged away to become a kitchen slave and the king gave the order for the smith to be flung face down and for the soldier to slice him across the back of the thighs with one sweep of his sword. The master craftsman was now hamstrung and henceforth would only shuffle and limp. Escape would be difficult for that prisoner and worse awaited. Wayland was taken to an island not far from the court, but far enough away to make swimming to shore impossible. There he was set to work to make treasures for his captors.

From time to time a boat would arrive with new supplies of precious metals and jewels to be fashioned into precious objects and with enough stores of food to sustain him. From time to time, Wayland's free brother contrived to be part of its crew or else messages were carried between servants and slaves, who had no reason to be loyal to their master other than through fear. So it was that the brothers managed to keep in touch, and all this time Wayland was plotting his escape. But escape alone was not enough for him, he also wanted revenge, and combining the two would not be easy. But at last his plan was ready.

He asked for an audience with the king and, after this long period of apparent docility, was granted it. There again was the king with the two princes on either hand, now almost young men. Nearby was the queen with their daughter, who modestly turned her blushing face away from this wonderous man, so strong and handsome above his maimed legs, a prisoner who was treated worse than their slaves, yet so noble in bearing.

Then Wayland showed why he had made his request and presented two surprise gifts he had made for the princes: perfectly balanced, exquisitely honed daggers, each with a handle shaped like a raven. That they represented the All Father's companions, Thought and Memory, who brought him news of what went on in the world of mortals, was lost on the youths. Like father, like son, greed lit up their eyes rather than any appreciation for the divine skill that had gone into their daggers' making. Wayland saw that his trap had been well set and smiled under his beard.

Before he returned to the island, he managed to get word to his brother to start collecting swan feathers from the shore and to find a way to smuggle them over to him in the supply boat. On that same night, the first snowfall of winter arrived. The flakes were huge and wet, the winter cold was not yet at its iciest. Unnoticed among the snowflakes was also a great fall of feathers. Wayland's beloved had summoned her sisters, who silently circled the shoreline, plucking out as many feathers as they could spare to help the captive brothers. With daylight the snow melted, but the feathers remained. It was not long before these had been gathered up and found their way to him hidden in sacks among the other supplies. It was then that Wayland bent his ingenuity to contriving a harness to which were attached huge wings made with those feathers. Under cover of darkness he would practise with it, the enormous strength in his smith's shoulders and arms lifting him high into the air. So he was now able to escape, but he was not yet ready to. Revenge was to come first.

Soon after he had a pair of clandestine visitors. The princes had been forbidden to visit him, yet here they were, a greasy gleam in their greedy eyes as they searched for other treasures that might become theirs. Perhaps they had some foolish notion of murdering the slave smith and stealing what they could, because their hands constantly played about their new daggers. Wayland noticed but did not say anything, other than that his best work lay in a chest at the back of the forge. Perhaps the young men would like to choose something for themselves? The young men certainly would. They bent over the chest, peering for treasure, not able in the gloom to see that it was empty. But it did not remain empty for long. Their daggers were not the only weapons that Wayland had made. One sweep of his hidden sword toppled both their heads into the chest.

It was too dangerous to keep their boat but it was a useful coffin for hiding the bodies. His immense strength made easy work of placing them in it and launching the boat with the bodies weighed down by stones. Pushing it before him as he waded out, one blow of his hammer left such a hole that it would soon be scuttled. Then a mighty shove pushed it even further into deep waters where it sank, never to be found.

Before long the search for the princes reached the island. There was the smith slave working away as usual, his fire hot, soup bubbling in a pot as he worked his bellows to melt more metal. He showed only surprise at the princes' disappearance – how could word have reached him in his prison before then? When the search party had left, he took the soup from where it hung over the fire and emptied it outside the forge. Inside the cauldron were the princes' skulls, now boiled clean of any flesh. The eyes he had removed and set aside, now he collected all the loosened teeth. Goblets were made of the skulls, richly rimmed and decorated with gold. Jewellery was made with the eyeballs and teeth. These were sent to the king and queen, who were delighted with them. They had no notion what these trinkets had been made from, and no notion that their sons were dead. No bodies had been found, so surely they had just gone off on some adventure as do many young men.

Wayland was now ready to leave – he had sent word to his brother to also make his escape, but then he received a visit he was not expecting. There was the princess, who had told her parents that she had broken her ring and wanted it repaired. Could not a servant have brought it here for her? Perhaps she hadn't told her parents at all and had sneaked over to the island as her brothers had done. Perhaps she had some inkling of their plan and had come for herself to see if there was some trace of them. Perhaps she had sought out the smith for himself and not for anything he could do for her. But there was her excuse, a ring she had deliberately broken that she was now holding out to him on her open palm. But Wayland was not looking at that ring, he was looking at the one she was wearing, the one he had made as a gift for his beloved swan maiden. At that moment the princess' fate was sealed.

The fire was not hot enough for such delicate work, so he would need to stoke it up. Would she please to take a seat for a while? Soon it was suffocatingly hot and they were both sweating. Perhaps she would take some beer, she must be getting thirsty. Gratefully she drank, but the girl was not used to such strong beer, and soon her head was spinning. It must be the heat making her dizzy – or was it drowsy – and she was so thirsty, so eager to drink more. When she was insensible, Wayland raped her, knowing as he did so that she would become pregnant. Revenge had turned an act of love into an act of hatred.

As darkness gathered people into the great hall, a huge white bird was seen circling it, the like of which had never been seen before. People were pointing at it, calling others to come and see. It was Wayland flying with the wings he had created from swan maiden feathers. In a huge voice he cried out for all to hear what he had done – how he had killed the princes, how their parents had been drinking from their skulls and flaunting jewels made from their eyes and teeth. Lastly he told of how he had left their sister pregnant and how the king's only heir would be a bastard fathered by rape. The king ordered his soldiers to loose their arrows and bring him down, but Wayland flew too high for them to reach. Then he flew fast and far away and was never seen by them again.

Cu Chulainn's Last Battle

The mightiest warrior that Ireland had ever known was waiting for the fighting to begin. He knew that this would be his greatest challenge yet, and he was ready for it. No sleep for him as that long night became a vigil. He shivered at the chill that crept through him, limning his bones, icy tongues licking at the very marrow of his will. Born to fight, he had never felt this way before a battle. As yet no hint of dawn drew the sounds of friend or foe reaching for their weapons. The silence was filled instead with images that appeared against the dark sky, that Cu Chulainn knew only he could see. They formed, shimmered and reformed like the colours that could sometimes be seen on a winter's night at the most northerly tip of the island. 'Lugh's dreams', the druids called them, when the God of Light slept his midwinter sleep in one of the sacred tombs that were the gateways between this and the Other World. Lugh was the god that people still whispered was Cu Chulainn's first father before his mother had married a mortal chieftain.

Were these visions, dreams or memories that played across his sight? There he saw himself as a youth defending Chullain the Smith's cattle, so fearless, so proud. How he ached to see himself so young, how he sorrowed again that his own son, inadvertently slain by his own hand, had not even reached that age. Unable to close his eyes against the sight that brought such anguish, he watched on as more of the story was revealed.

He saw a heifer being led away from the herd by a woman he did not recognise, a woman who was neither guest nor member of that clan. But this time, because he knew what would happen next, he cringed as the scene unfolded. Nevertheless, he reached out a hand to restrain his younger self; to place a warning touch on that shoulder although he knew that he was helpless to reach into the past. How he wished now that he could roll back the certainty and arrogance of youth as he heard his voice rough with challenge instead of gentle with greeting. How certain and contemptuous was his tone as he accused her of stealing the beast. She denied that she was a thief but still he persisted, instead of asking courteously who she was and why he could perhaps be making a mistake. Had he done so he would have learned that he was talking to The Morrigan herself, Earth goddess, warrior goddess, reader of the fates of all those who now flourished in Ireland since the Fomorian giants had been defeated with her help. Guardian of the land and all the animals that thrived upon it, how could she be stealing one over which she held sovereignty?

The vision was relentless: Cu Chulainn launched himself at the woman to seize her but she turned herself into a crow and flew up into a branch, whence she fixed him with a round, implacable glare. It was only then that he realised who he was dealing with. The Sovereign Goddess of the land favoured shifting into the shape of a crow, especially when foretelling a warrior's doom. He told her that if had he realised who she was, he would have spoken differently and did not want to part as enemies. Insulted and angered, The Morrigan in her crow form insisted that his fate had been sealed in any case. Ever incapable of resisting a challenge, contrition instantly changed to defiance as the youth declared that he could not be defeated. Nevertheless in the vision, Cuchullain was forced to hear again the threatening words that followed, foretelling how The Morrigan would be both author of, and companion to, his fate.

Now it seemed that lightning flashes were flickering above him, but the warrior recognised them as the flames of the fire he had seen when travelling to the battlefield. There again he saw the three old women who beckoned him over to taste the stew they were cooking. Cu Chulainn did not want to delay and hurried on, but they called after him. He should never have turned back, but just as giving hospitality was the law of the land, so was accepting it, especially when he had been invited three times. In his haste he did not ask himself how these crones could look so alike, why the fire seemed to be burning without any fuel, why there was no scent of the food bubbling in the pot. For form's sake, he gulped down a mouthful. Something stuck between his teeth – it was another tooth – the unmistakeable canine from a dog.

As he watched that scene that he had so recently experienced, his gut heaved with revulsion. It was taboo for him to eat dog meat, ever since his destiny had been shaped by an encounter with a monstrous hound, which he had killed when it attacked him. Since then, against his will, his own name had been changed to one that described him as having taken the place of the owner's dog. Forbidden ever after to eat dog meat, he now realised that breaking the taboo was the worst possible omen. Unassailable by any mortal, he had been tricked into weakening his power with that one act.

A last vision appeared. There was the ford where he was now standing, and which he was to defend on the following day. But now he saw it as he had first approached it, saw himself hesitate, peer into the gloom at a shape he could not clearly make out at first. The figure huddled at the water's edge, and there were splashing sounds above the murmuring of the flow. Then the clouds had parted. In the moonlight he had seen an old woman kneeling, kneading something in the water. As she raised her face he recognised her as one of the three crones who had tricked him into eating dog flesh, but as he watched her eyes became round and gold bright, her nose hooked as a beak. The cloth hung pale in her hands as she lifted it to let the water stream from it. Even at night the warrior could recognise blood stains. No matter how much she pummelled and squeezed it, the blood remained, and Cuchullain recognised the garment she was washing as his own shirt.

Dawn brought the moment for the last battle to commence. Fighting would be a relief after those ill-omened visions. Ireland's mightiest warrior readied himself to meet the enemy's heroes in single combat by the ford. He would fight alone as only he had escaped the Earth goddesses' ancient curse preventing warriors from fighting for five days. There was an unaccountable lull after the long night of waiting. Perhaps none of the others wanted to be the first to take him on. Then there was movement as a figure approached, not another warrior, but an exquisite woman who offered Cuchullain her help, her company and comfort. He was furious at this distraction, demanding to know why she couldn't see that he had more important things on his mind than dallying with some female. Again he had insulted The Morrigan, too late he realised who he had been speaking to so dismissively.

Their next encounter was one of open hostility as, while he was fighting waist deep in the ford, she shape-shifted into a giant eel that twisted between his thighs, trying to bring him down before his opponent. He managed nevertheless to win that encounter and also succeeded in wounding the monster. The Morrigan came at him again in the shape of a wolf, stampeding a herd of cattle across the ford to crush him. Again he escaped her enmity and wounded her again in her wolf form. Swiftly she became the leader of the herd trying to trample him. Again he escaped and not before she had sustained yet another wound.

Time passed. Many enemy heroes would not return to take back their stones from the cairns that they had built, each one adding a stone before they went into battle. The stones that remained would show how many had been killed when the fighting was over at last. But The Morrigan did not count stones, if she counted anything it was souls.

While enemy forces regrouped, Cuchullain noticed that he was thirsty and even a little tired. He had never noticed any discomforts before when he was still in fighting mode. His eyes lingered with longing on a cow that was being driven by an old woman, so old that she was limping and hobbling. She stopped nearby and at first he thought it was her frailty that made her rest. But no, she was milking her cow and he was glad to see that she was offering him a bowl of milk. Gratefully he took it and blessed her for her kindness. Three times she offered and three times he accepted, blessing her each time before he drank. Then the old woman drew back her hood and swept to her feet, towering straight and strong above him. The Morrigan thanked Cuchullain for those blessings because, at each one, a wound that he had given her at the ford had healed, and she was now whole again.

He had been tired before this last encounter with the goddess and by now it was clear that his greatest enemy was sleep. Fatigue weighed his eyelids, blurred his vision, slowed his limbs and brought weakness to his grip on spear or sword. Time had become a bloody blur, and it would not be long before he would be caught falling into the arms of his next opponent, sleep taken before any weapon touched him. But as he swayed drowsily against his spear, he was not alone. There at his side appeared his father, his first and divine father, come among mortals once more as he had done to conceive him, his half mortal, half divine son. Lugh, God of Light, shone with the battle light that Cu Chulainn was known for and which he had inherited. It was Lugh who now fought his son's would-be slayers, holding them at bay so that his son could sleep at last. On he slept while his father held the battleground, Lugh all the while knowing that he could not change his son's fate but that at least he could delay it.

6

THE PASSING OF THE IMMORTALS

In the time
In the time when
In the time when the darkness created all things
The Sun was created
The Sun is born, and dies, and comes again

In the time
In the time when
In the time when the darkness created all things
The Moon was created
The Moon is born, and dies, and comes again

In the time
In the time when
In the time when the darkness created all things
The Stars were created
The Stars are born, and die, and come again

In the time
In the time when
In the time when the darkness created all things
We were created

We are born, and die, and may not come again

Sharon Jacksties, 'Diana's Daughters'

THE DEATH OF CU CHULLAINN

Whether we fall by ambition, blood or lust,
Like diamonds, we are cut with our own dust.

Webster

Cu Chulainn's long years of fighting had made him many mortal enemies, but the worst of these was Queen Maeve, whose champion he had been but who now blamed him for not winning the war that she had started purely out of greed and envy. Her desire for revenge was as compelling as her greed. She nurtured six children whom Cu Chulainn had made fatherless in battle, welcoming them to her court, ensuring that they were given the best education with the most skilled of the druids. At the end of their seven years of training, they had made three magical spears that their druid teacher prophesied would each kill a king.

These were given as weapons to Lugaid, the brother who showed the most promise in Maeve's eyes. The first spear killed Cu Chulainn's charioteer, who was so skilled that he was known as a king among charioteers. Thus was the first of the prophecies fulfilled. The next spear killed his horse, a matchless beast who was known as the king of the horses, and so the second prophecy came to pass. How could the third fail? The last spear pierced Cu Chulainn, king among warriors, so that his intestines spilled out, mortally wounding him. Knowing that he was about to die, the champion used them to tie himself to a pillar so that he would die upright rather than fall before his enemies.

Still Lugaid was too cautious to approach Cu Chulainn. It was one thing to throw a spear from a distance, another to be within reach of that sword arm. Finally a crow alighted on the champion's shoulder, glared all around with her fierce yellow eyes, raised her beak and cawed in triumph. Only then was Lugaid certain that his enemy was dead and, lunging forward, he cut off his head with one stroke. A blaze of light burst from Cu Chulainn's corpse, framing it, reaching towards the sky as his spirit joined his father, Lugh, God of Light. His sword dropped from his hand, severing that of his slayer as it fell. The light blazed on until his sword arm too was cut off, and all was darkness until his story was told.

THE COMING OF WISDOM

Before time was new, there was only an abyss of nothing. Then appeared a realm of shadows without form or colour or substance. Emerging from the shadows came waters, fire, wind and ice. From this melting ice was born the first being, the Giant Ymir. His children were created from his sweat and born in his armpit. Other creatures emerged from the ice, including another being whose son mated with the giant's daughter, who bore three children. That was how the race of gods and goddesses was born. The eldest of these was the god Odin, All Father, who would become the chief of the gods. It was his race that set the celestial bodies in what had become the sky, and ordered their journeys. It was then that time was new.

Many different beings had been created, some living in harmony, some in strife. Not long after they had appeared, the gods and goddesses had made enemies of the giants through their own greed and treachery. After countless aeons battling with giants and monsters, this was to lead to their downfall – the end of the world as they had known it, to be consumed by war and fire. But that would be when their time was old, and, for now, everything that was to make up their worlds had appeared in its beauty, its variety and its terrifying power.

There stood the great ash tree, Yggdrasil, centre of all creation, its trunk stretching through all the Other Worlds from the roots of existence itself to the highest reaches of the sky. Beneath one of its roots was the world of frost and ice where the giants lived. Beneath their world was a fountain that ran with the waters of wisdom. How Odin desired to be truly wise, how he yearned to be able to know all that was happening in the many worlds – those of the divine beings, the giants, the dwarves, the monsters and the humans. How he wanted to use wisdom for the benefit of his race and the puny humans they protected.

The fountain had a guardian, Mimir the Wise, whose name meant 'The One Who Remembers'. He gained his knowledge from drinking the waters of the fountain and he was one whom Odin admired greatly. If it could be said that Odin had a friend, it was Mimir, but even so his friend was not able to simply let Odin drink those magical waters. A price would have to be paid. You get nothing for nothing, even if you are a god, even if you are the chief of the gods, and if Odin wanted to drink from the fountain of wisdom, it would cost him. He was already wise enough to know that the greater the price, the more he would gain. So it was that Odin plucked out his right eye and threw it into the fountain, where it remained. Moreover, he also inflicted on himself a greater sacrifice: plunging his divine spear into his side. Then, wounded and in agony, he hung himself in the branches of Yggdrasil for nine days and nine nights without eating or drinking. His self-inflicted suffering through pain, hunger and thirst brought on visions that taught him, among many skills, the healing arts, the power to shape-shift and, finally, the discovery of the runes and how to use them. These characters were not merely an alphabet, but also held magical meanings and the power to cast spells.

When he had recovered from his ordeal, Odin had gained the ability to see what was happening in all the worlds and into the future. He was accompanied by two ravens named Thought and Memory – the latter perhaps to honour his friend Mimir. Odin would send them to spy out what was happening in distant places and to come back and report what they had seen, because of course by now Odin could understand the speech of all the animals and the birds. When his friend was decapitated in one of the many wars between the gods and the giants, Odin found his body and preserved his head with his knowledge of healing herbs. In this way he was able to keep Mimir's head alive and it would whisper secrets and advice to him when he carried it about.

Odin is always described as having one eye and people think of his all-seeing knowledge as a reward for his willingness to pluck it out as part of his sacrifice. But we forget that his eye was lying at the very source of the fountain whose waters granted that wisdom. There it lay perpetually bathed by those magical waters and it was through that eye that Odin saw all. It was through the absent eye that the All Father saw what was denied to others.

Not so long ago this was still understood by the people of Orkney who until recent times venerated the Odin Stone or, as it was also called, 'The Eye of Odin'. Their islands had been ruled by Norsemen who believed the old religion with Odin's story at its heart. Hundreds of years after the new religion of Christianity had come to Orkney, with its own version of the All Father's sacrifice, this stone was still being venerated. It was the site of many rituals and traditions until the early twentieth century. There it stood, slightly apart from the sacred Stones of Stenness, a standing stone with the distinction of having a round hole some 3ft from its base. This gap symbolised Odin's missing eye and when people looked through it, it was as though they too were seeing the unseeable, granted a vision from Other Worlds. It was there that people went to see into the impenetrable, to use magical means to reveal what was hidden to mortal sight. Despite the proliferation of the Bible, oaths sworn and promises made while touching the stone, or with hands clasped through Odin's missing eye, were considered to be more binding than any other. More than one thousand years after the advent of Christianity, in 1784, the Reverend Henry noted:

There was a custom among the lower class of people in this country. The parties agreed stole from the rest of their companions, and went to the Temple of the Moon [Stones of Stenness], where the woman, in presence of the man, fell down on her knees and prayed to the god Wodden (for such was the name of the god they addressed upon this occasion) that he would enable her to perform all the promises and obligations she had and was to make to the young man present, after which they both went to the Temple of the Sun [Ring of Brodgar], where the man prayed in like manner before the woman, then they repaired from this to the stone [known as Wodden's or Odin's

Stone], and the man being on one side and the woman on the other, they took hold of each other's right hand through the hole, and there swore to be constant and faithful to each other.

So it was that, for centuries, the practices of the old religion endured side by side with the new. It was in the early nineteenth century that the stone was felled by an unpopular incomer. This act alone drew the hatred of the local people. Not content with this destruction, he set about pulling down the nearby Stones of Stenness, until neighbours intervened and he was prevented. The piece with Odin's missing eye somehow survived, lying forgotten on the farmland until the 1940s, when the son of the farmer decided to have a clear out. He was unaware of what it was, or what it had been. Not being able to move it, he broke it into many pieces, and was sworn at by his father for having done so. The farmer had never been able to look through its eye as it had lain flat on the ground throughout his life. He had never been able to see with Odin's wisdom into the mysteries of other worlds and so had neglected to mention anything of its holy properties to the next generation.

MERLIN ENCHANTED

How could it happen that the greatest wizard ever known in these islands allowed himself to be enchanted by one of his own apprentices? When Nimue came to Camelot everyone sensed that here was no ordinary mortal, with her faraway look, her gliding, silent presence, her ability to see into everyone's inner thoughts. More than once she had managed to save King Arthur's life, some even joked that she was the Lady of the Lake herself who had come among them. Some did not join in the smiles as they half believed it to be true.

Soon there was more joking, but always behind his back, that Merlin the Enchanter was himself under her spell. Surely that grey figure, older far than any at court, was too old to be in love? But everyone could see how devoted he was to her, following Nimue as though he were her own grey shadow. Most thought it was a case of that least dignified of love triangles, Youthful Beauty, Ugly Old Age and Infatuation. Nobody ever asked whether Nimue ever returned Merlin's love, and for Merlin, that was all to the good.

All basked in the warm glow of Camelot's golden age. So pleasant had their lives become that few remembered those perilous times that, without Merlin, would never have grown into this period of peace and plenty. Now Nimue, Arthur's protector, was among them. Had her magical powers not discovered every plot against him? Only recently she had detected the malign enchantment in a gift sent as an apology for a failed attack on one of his knights, but this time the target was Arthur himself. It was Nimue who insisted that the bearer of the gift try on that gloriously shimmering robe before the king touched it. Not knowing how to avoid this unexpected turn of events, the servant had put it on and was covered by an even greater brightness as the robe burst into all-consuming flames, leaving only ashes to return to her treacherous mistress.

So it was that some pitied and some sneered as Merlin's infatuation led him to treat Nimue as he had never before treated any of his former pupils, teaching her his secret arts, adding his magical powers to hers. Perhaps it suited him that people believed he was doing this as a way to find favour in the eyes of the one he adored. Perhaps Merlin had another purpose. Able to see into the future, his own as well as that of others, he knew the occasion when he would last see Arthur, and made his farewells accordingly.

Surely he also knew the fate that awaited Arthur, the fate that had also been shaped by Arthur's shape-shifting half-sister, she who had borne Arthur's son who would become his nemesis. Surely Merlin knew that Arthur would be killed by him in this world, and taken by the priestesses, servants of the Goddess, to the Other World. There, still sleeping, to be healed by them, until it was time for him to returned to ours. And when that time, however distant, came at last, who would there be to protect and advise him then?

Merlin was by now the oldest of the old.

He too would need to fall into an enchanted sleep if he were to follow his king, awakening into that other time yet to come. But who would have the power to charm a magician such as himself with a spell so strong that it could endure through ages, protecting him from enemies and nurturing the half-life of sleep until he was needed once more?

Nimue was such a one and so Merlin added his power and knowledge to hers until her art equalled or excelled his own. It was then that her spell was cast and Merlin, caught in the web of his own weaving, was bound finally to his last hiding place and his last sleep. There he lies until his destiny wakes him once more. Some say he is hidden in a tower, others a cave, a hollow tree or beneath a great slab of stone, and the less we mortals know, the safer he is against our meddling.

BALDUR BETRAYED

Baldur the Radiant, Baldur the Beloved, was the son of the rulers of all the gods and goddesses. His mother was Frigg, and his father was her consort, Odin. Baldur brought joy to every company. As soon as he appeared, argument melted away, enemies nodded to each other and it was as though the sun itself were shining inside the great halls of the divine throng. As he was the most popular of all the gods, he had nothing to fear. Why then was he looking so pale and uncertain, jumping at the slightest noise or sudden movement? At last he mentioned that he had been troubled by bad dreams in which an unknown assassin was trying to kill him, but in his dream he could not tell by which means. As he spoke, Frigg's face became graver. It transpired that she too had been having these same dreams about Baldur. This double omen could not be ignored, and Odin, in his wisdom, took it most seriously.

Despite his great wisdom, or maybe because of it, Odin knew that certain of the divinatory arts were best practised by women, so he decided to consult a visionary, one who had been a noted seer and a prophetess. Although there were many he could have visited, this particular one had excelled at her art, but she was now dead. Odin too had great powers, and among those at his command were the power of the runes. He resolved to enter the Underworld to use the runes to practise necromancy – the art of raising the dead – in order to question the greatest seer that had ever lived. Odin knew that if he were successful, she would be bound to answer every question she was asked, as those who were summoned from the dead always appeared unwillingly and, desperate to be released from the spell, would be compliant so that they could return to their graves the sooner.

Odin mounted his eight-legged steed, Sleipnir. This horse was a result of yet another of Loki's misdemeanours, a by-product of one of the trickster god's punishments. Odin urged Sleipnir to gallop to Hel, the realm of the dead where all remained unless they had died gloriously in battle. Realising that he was likely to find out more if no one knew that he was enquiring about his own son, Odin decided to disguise himself. He hid Sleipnir close by, so as not to draw any untoward attention, and approached the gates of Hel. These were guarded by a fearsome hound who would not let the living enter, nor the dead depart. He was not fooled by any disguise and instantly recognised Odin, but made the right decision not to challenge him.

As soon as he was past the gates, Odin noticed that preparations were being made for some great banquet as though to welcome an important guest – although whoever it was would never be leaving. He had never seen such lavish preparations, but there were more urgent things to attend to. His necromancy succeeded in summoning the dead and the seer's remains shambled towards him through the gloom. Her sightless eyes tried to look into his one eye, hidden beneath his broad-brimmed hat, as she asked him who he was.

'They call me "Wanderer" madam,' which was not entirely a lie as Odin was known to wander through all the worlds in his quest for knowledge.

But the mystery of the extravagant banquet persisted. The need to know the identity of the guest who commanded such honour seemed to obscure all else. So Odin's first question was to know who the feast was being prepared for. In his heart of hearts he already knew the answer, but when the seer whispered his son's name, his heart thrashed inside him like a seal caught in a net. He struggled not to let his distress weaken the power he needed to maintain his necromancer's magic. He had to keep this corpse under his spell, conjuring her anew each time he asked a question, so bent was she on returning to her eternal rest. Each reply was dragged out of her as she gasped her answers in a voice as rough as sharkskin. Each time she answered she reproached him for making her reply under duress. With each answer, she begged to be allowed to return to her grave – but there was more for Odin to learn: his beloved son Baldur would be killed by his own twin brother, and his death would be avenged by yet another of Odin's sons – one who was not yet born, but who would nevertheless exact his revenge within a day of his birth. When he heard this, Odin was so distraught that he insulted the seer, and at that momentary loss of control she was able to summon her own power for her riposte. It was that she would never again benefit anyone with her second sight until the ending of all the worlds, and that would not be long in coming.

Odin rode from Hel with tormented thoughts. If it was not possible to avert his son's fate, then it was unthinkable that his death would go unavenged. But if the seer's visions were true, whenever he sired the boy who would be his son's avenger, it would mean that Baldur would die nine months and a day afterwards and Odin himself would be weaving a thread in the web of Baldur's fate. Just as his heart had felt like a seal trapped in a net, now it was his thoughts that were thrashing to escape his mind and flee into action. When he returned home, he spoke to Frigg, who called a council of all the gods and goddesses. Not everything that Odin had learned was shared with that divine gathering; he did not mention the prophesied roles of Baldur's brothers. All the gods and goddesses were present and all were asked to promise never to harm Baldur. Even the trickster god, Loki the treacherous, unhesitatingly swore that solemn oath, 'I swear I will never raise my hand against him.'

All the other deities sighed with relief. They knew that among them all, Loki was least to be trusted. Frigg then announced that she would travel throughout the worlds and ask every being and everything to take the same oath that they would never harm Baldur. This seemed the best and indeed the only plan, and Frigg wasted no time in setting out on her mission.

Only the world of the dead remained unvisited – that place from which none would ever be permitted to emerge to kill her beloved son. With a mother's patience and fortitude, Frigg journeyed throughout the worlds speaking to all their various beings, marvellous or monstrous, and all without hesitation pledged never to harm him. Even the giants, who had no reason to love the gods, willingly gave their promises. To say that she left no stone unturned would be to reclaim a cliché. Everything to be found in the natural world, whether earth, sand, stones, boulders or mountains were requested to take the same oath. Most powerful of all the goddesses, Frigg was able to grant them all the ability to hear, to understand and to speak their pledges. Ice promised not to freeze or trap Baldur, snow promised not to crush or suffocate him in an avalanche, water not to drown or choke him, fire not to burn or suffocate him with smoke. And so it went on as she moved through the whole of creation.

At last the deed was done, and, relieved, she returned to her divine realm. Baldur was no longer troubled by those ominous dreams and neither was his mother. Odin and Frigg had done all they could to protect their son, and Odin absented himself to rekindle a former dalliance with a giantess. So much more pleasant to be making love than war. Meanwhile, the other gods and goddesses were filled with delight at Baldur's reprieve. It was time to celebrate, and joyfully they set about devising games and entertainments. Playing was so much more fun than fighting giants.

Perhaps because of its novelty, their favourite game was 'Who can hurt Baldur?'. Knowing that this was now an impossibility, his companions became more and more inventive in their methods of attack. There he would stand in a circle while his laughing assailants would hurl missiles at him. These could be conventional weapons, such as spears, which just glanced off him without even marking his skin – for had not all metals sworn not to harm him? But by now his friends were being more amusingly creative, strangling him with horse's reins that just disintegrated as they touched him, hurling adders at him that coiled harmlessly around his limbs and slid away. And so their sport went on and it seemed that so great was their relief at danger passing, that they would never tire of it.

Perhaps relief had surpassed caution with Frigg, when a stranger came to her hall. The law of hospitality ensured a welcome to all and Frigg invited the old woman to sit by the fire. Preoccupied with other matters, Frigg spoke to her and answered her question out of politeness, though her mind was elsewhere.

The stranger explained that she lived alone in a remote place and so she always felt that she was the last to hear any news. She had given her oath not to hurt Baldur some time ago, but was it really true that Great Frigg had managed to ask and receive the same from everybody and everything? Even those that were inanimate? What a relief, what a saving grace! But could she be absolutely certain that she had missed nothing out? How could she be so sure? At this Frigg hesitated because there was just one thing she hadn't asked to swear – something so insignificant and so young, it was too immature to be able to take an oath. It was as though her guest had noticed this hesitation, and for the first time for a long while, Frigg was visited by a cold shiver of fear, but the old woman continued to ramble on, as old women do, and the moment passed.

'I am sure you were right Greatest Goddess, and what was this young thing, exactly, just to reassure you that you need have no qualms?'

'It was just a little sprig of mistletoe growing on an oak branch, Old One, so pale and delicate, it didn't even have any berries yet, I could hardly even make it out in the dusk …' Frigg heard her words gathering pace as her tone grew more anxious. Why did she sound as though she were apologising?'

'Quite so, Great Frigg, a sprig of mistletoe, how sweet, how very sweet.'

The old woman had risen and was walking far more briskly toward the door than she had when she came through it. On the threshold she stopped and turned.

'Thank you Greatest Goddess, thank you for everything.'

And Frigg did not know that she had been speaking to Loki the treacherous, shape-shifted into the form of an old woman to find out what he needed to know.

Loki wasted no time. He found a healthy bunch of mistletoe and selected its strongest stem. This he attached to the end of his spear, and then he was ready. Joining the throng of goddesses and gods who were still playing their favourite game of 'Who can hurt Baldur?' he made his way to Hodur, Baldur's twin, who was standing apart.

'Not playing, my friend, why is that?'

Loki knew full well that Hodur was not playing because he was blind and could not see the target.

'What would be the point when I cannot see? I am more likely to hit one of the other players and bring enmity or a blood feud on myself. I am surprised, Loki, that you, with all your cunning, should ask such a foolish question.'

A pity that his surprise did not lead him to wonder what might have been behind it. But all the goddesses and gods knew that there was no danger, had they not proved it time and time again in their play?

'Not at all, I can help you to join in the game. Let me stand behind you. Here, take my spear. You can feel that I have already protected its point so that you can't hurt yourself with it. Perhaps your fingers will recognise the mistletoe around it. I will take your arm and guide it so that you are pointing at the target. When you feel my grip tighten you will know that you are perfectly placed and you can let fly with all your strength.'

No longer an outsider, able to join in at last, Hodur let fly the spear at Loki's signal. With all the pent up strength and frustration of a god who had never been allowed to bear weapons because of his blindness, that spear was thrown unerringly, rendered lethal by means of a harmless-looking plant. There was a second when it was flying, during which Loki melted away into the crowd. Then Baldur fell down dead. Everyone had seen who had done it and Loki, treacherous trickster god, had kept his oath. It had been Hodur's hand that he had raised against Baldur, not his own. In another part of creation, in the world of the giants, a giantess was giving birth to Hodur's brother, who avenged that death within the same day – just as had been prophesised.

There lay Baldur's body burning on the ceremonial funeral pyre that had been assembled on his boat. His vessel was the largest that had ever been built. Nearby was the body of his twin, Hodur, his innocent assassin. Every creature in all the worlds, apart from Loki, was mourning. He was awaiting his punishment, which he had always known would come. Even though it would involve the death of his own sons, for Loki it would all have been worth it. How he sneered when Baldur's immense boat proved too large to be pushed into the sea for its final voyage. There it rested onshore with its burning burdens, for some had thrown themselves on the funeral blaze rather than live without him. So great was everyone's grief that enmity between giants and gods and goddesses had been forgotten. At last a giantess appeared riding on a giant wolf, her reins writhing snakes. With her immense strength she pushed the boat into the tide. For a moment there was fire under, as well as upon it, as her powerful shove struck sparks from beneath its keel.

For a long time, nobody and nothing moved, even after the last lick of flame had been swallowed by the ocean. Any world without Baldur was unimaginable. That is why he would have to be returned to them. Frigg was not going to give up and the Goddess of the Underworld, who was also called Hel just like the realm she ruled over, would be petitioned. In a voice loud with the force of anguish, so that it could be heard throughout all the worlds, Frigg announced that this would be so. Again Loki sneered, Hel had never before surrendered any of those over whom she ruled – moreover, she was his own daughter.

Odin was so weighed down with grief that Sleipnir couldn't carry him. Frigg couldn't bear to retrace her steps past all those beings who had remained faithful to their promises – they were too painful a reminder of her loss. Hermod, another of Baldur's brothers, volunteered to be their messenger and was sent to Hel. There, with her guard dog safely under her control, he was given an audience on the threshold of Hel itself. First Hermod used the argument that as Odin, a living being, had both entered and departed in order to conjure the dead seer, a precedent had already been set and someone should be allowed to leave Hel. The goddess replied that, as she had lost someone who should have remained having once crossed her threshold, perhaps the messenger would like to take his place? It was clear that sophistry was not going to work. Hermod then described how everything and everybody that had been asked to swear an oath not to harm Baldur had agreed, and how he had only been harmed by the one thing that hadn't been asked to make that promise.

'Did all things and beings make that promise except for one, and that merely because it wasn't asked? Well if that is true, I will offer you this one chance to win back Baldur and it should not be a difficult task. Many tears are shed for my guests who will never return, but never has all of creation wept for only one of them. If all the beings and things in creation will weep for Baldur when they are asked, then I will return him.'

Hermod hastened back with this happy news and messengers ranged through all the worlds to ask every being and every thing to weep for Baldur, and it seemed that all were willing. For the first and only time, even stones wept salt tears and flames wept in dark gouts. But then, at last, there was one who refused to weep – Loki again, but now disguised as a giantess, 'Why should I weep for Baldur when he killed my three sons? Let Goddess Hel keep what she has!'

At that, all hope was lost, and with it Baldur the Radiant, Baldur the Beloved, until soon after, when all the known worlds were destroyed and Baldur, his twin brother and his avenging brother were all reborn into the new.

The Fairy Piper

Something new was moving across Ireland. Like a strange wind that made people turn towards it, tilting their heads in a different direction to catch this new murmuring, the people knew that change was coming. It was not only the mortals, however, the old gods and goddesses were stirring uneasily as they dozed, and the fairy folk were as restless as they were wary.

It was said that a man was among them with magical powers, even with divine powers, some whispered, and his name was

Patrick. This Patrick spoke of One more powerful than all the known divinities combined, One whose power encompassed all that could be imagined and more. Throughout the land Patrick travelled, preaching about this new religion until some believed, some clung to the old beliefs, some believed both, and some did not know what to believe.

Patrick was in a district where few could scratch a living from the poor soil and the treacherous moors. He was staying at a remote farmhouse when he received a message from a family who had embraced his teachings. One of their elders was dying and asking for Patrick to administer the last rites. The messenger had taken days to find him, so there was no time to be lost. But how was Patrick to find a way across the moors in the dark? Not even the local people would dare such a journey. But Patrick was desperate to reach one of the few families he had managed to convert and was determined to make the attempt. When his host saw that he could not be dissuaded, he said, 'Well you will just have to trust to the good will of the fairy piper to guide you across the moor.'

He went on to explain that if ever anybody was desperate enough to cross the moor at night, they had to wait by the sacred stone and hope that their presence would summon the fairy piper. If they were lucky they would then hear the music of the bagpipes in the darkness, and if they followed the sound, their guide from the Other World would see them safely across that treacherous waste. Then he took up a lantern and said that he would take Patrick to the holy stone, which was to be found close by – indeed, how would the generations have survived without it?

In the lamplight Patrick could see a tall sliver of stone that stood like a vertical bridge between earth and sky. For all its slenderness it seemed to hold a great weight as though there were as much below ground as above. In the flickering lantern light, it seemed to weave a dance between light and shadow.

'I will leave you here now. It is not respectful for me to linger, the need not being my own. Good luck with your journey, and whenever you return make sure you only travel in daylight.'

Patrick had only been there for moments when the sky cleared and a waxing moon shone out over the midnight stillness. Despite the sudden brightness, now the stark contrast between light and dark made judging distance difficult. Gilded shadows pooled over the ground and all was shimmering silver or oily black. It was impossible to make out what might be dry ground or the damp gleam that hinted at the dangerous bogs lurking beneath. Then a sudden wind swept scudding clouds across the moon and the chase between cloud dark and moonlight confused his sight. He resolved to take his host's advice, hoping that the fairy piper would appear rather than venturing on alone. There he stood, bewildered by the vast space and the changing light, when suddenly he was no longer alone.

Had the figure stepped out from behind that great standing stone? Patrick did not want to admit to himself that he had seen the man emerging *from inside it.*

Tall he stood under a sky that was suddenly empty of clouds again, and the two looked at each other, except that Patrick had the distinct impression that the fairy piper was looking *through* and *past* him. In the stillness it seemed that he too was made of stone. The only movement was in the glitter of moonlight that drew cold sparks from his eyes and played about the curious brooch that pinned his cloak. In that cold light, Patrick could see that all were a deep, vibrant green.

'I will guide you safely, mortal, to the dying man you seek, but I will also ask that you do something for me.'

Patrick was at first too surprised to answer. How did this being know what his mission was? Should he agree, knowing how his people had fallen foul of any bargains with the fairy folk, or would it be unchancy to refuse?

'Before he passes from your world into the Other World, I want you to ask him a question on behalf of all my people.'

Now Patrick felt a little easier. In those days it was well known that those about to die, who were lingering on the threshold between this and the Other World, could see beyond what was known in the mortal realm. If they were asked a question that could only be answered by the wisdom that lay beyond, they were bound to answer.

'We hear about a new god that has come to this land. One who is greater than all the gods and goddesses of all the worlds. They say that his power is able to change the Immortals into mortals just like your people. Although we cannot age, some of my people are growing tired. Ask, therefore, if ever we are able to die as you are, whether we too will be able to attain what you call the Kingdom of Heaven.'

Patrick agreed to ask the question. The moon was suddenly covered by clouds, which did not scud past as before so all was consumed by darkness. In the distance, the sound of the pipes swooped and soared over the moors. Patrick would have wondered how they could be coming from so far away in so short a time if he had not been instantly spellbound by the beauty of their music. It spoke to him of every longing the soul could feel, of greater joys and sorrows than a mortal heart could bear. He stood listening, transfixed, forgetting his purpose. It was only when that fairy music drew so far away that it became hard to hear that Patrick remembered why he was there. He hastened after the sound, blundering off in its direction in as straight a course as was possible.

For the rest of that night he followed the music, never getting any closer but managing to keep its elusive sweet strains just within earshot. When dawn paled the sky, the pipes fell silent and Patrick was within sight of the village where lay the dying man. He was just in time to administer the last rites and to ask the fairy piper's question. He attended the burial and the wake and then it was time to return. Patrick remembered the advice not to cross the moors at night, but how then would he be able to find the standing stone in the dark and keep his promise to his guide? He tried to time his journey so that he would reach it at nightfall, and this he managed to do.

The night was cloudless and as he waited, a full moon rose over the moor. When its silver touch stroked the stone, its surface shimmered and the fairy piper appeared.

'What is the answer to my question, mortal?'

'The dying man said that if there is one drop of human blood in you or yours, you may attain the Kingdom of Heaven. If there is none, then that world will always remain closed to you.'

At that, the fairy piper unclasped the curious brooch that Patrick had noticed before. It flashed silver fire in the moonlight as the fairy piper jabbed it into the ball of his thumb. Then he held his hand to the light as he squeezed out his blood, which ran clear gold in a thin stream.

'If we are not wanted in your Heaven, then neither will we be helping you on this Earth and the fairy piper will be heard no more.'

It was just as those bitter words had said. From that night until this night, the moors lost their guide. Many a human life has been lost on them since then. Great sorrow though that is, some say that it is a greater sorrow to have lost the fairy music forever.

BIBLIOGRAPHY

BOOKS

Branston, Brian, *The Lost Gods of England* (Book Club Associates, by arrangement with Thames and Hudson Ltd, London, 1974).

Branston, Brian, *Gods and Heroes from Viking Mythology* (London: Eurobook Ltd, 1978).

Conlee, John, ed., *Prose Merlin* (Western Michigan University, 1998).

Douglas, Amy, *Shropshire Folk Tales* (Stroud: The History Press, 2011).

Geddes, *Celtic Mythology* (Geddes & Grosset, 1999).

Geoffrey of Monmouth, *The History of the Kings of Britain* (London: Penguin Books Ltd, 1966).

Geoffrey of Monmouth, *Vita Merlinae* (ReadaClassic.com, 2011).

Giraldus Cambrensis, *Topographica Hibernia* (*c.* 1146).

Graves, Robert, *The White Goddess* (Manchester: Faber & Faber, 1999).

Hillaby, John, *Journey through Britain* (Paladin, 1970).

Jacksties, Sharon, *Animal Folk Tales of Britain and Ireland* (Cheltenham: The History Press, 2020).

Jones, Gwyn, and Jones, Thomas (trans.), *The Mabinogion* (London: Everyman, 2001).

Lady Gregory, *A Treasury of Irish Myth, Legend and Folklore* (New York: Avenel Books, 1986).

Larousse, *New Encyclopaedia of Mythology* (Paris: Librairie Larousse, 1968).

Mackenzie, Donald, *Scottish Wonder Tales from Myth and Legend* (New York: Dover Publications Inc., 1997).

MacKillop, James, *Myths and Legends of the Celts* (London: Penguin Books, 2005).

Malory, Tomas, *Le Morte d'Arthur*.

Ó hÓgáin, Dáithí, *The Lore of Ireland* (Woodbridge, Suffolk: The Boydell Press, 2006).

Parker, Will, *The Four Branches of the Mabinogi: Celtic Myth and Medieval Reality* (Bardic Press, 2007), www.mabinogi.net/fourbranches.html?sections/Appendix/Rigantona.pdf

Penguin Classics, *Early Irish Myths and Sagas* (London: Penguin, 1981).

Sturluson Snorri, *Prose Edda*.

Stewart, R.J., *Celtic Gods and Celtic Goddesses* (London: Blandford, 1990).

Virgil, *The Aeneid* (London: Penguin Classics, 1969).

Wilson, H. Hay, *Forgotten Books* (New York: J.M. Dent and Sons Ltd, 1912).

WEBSITES

www.mabinogi.net/fourbranches.html?sections/Appendix/
    Rigantona.pdf

Academy of Ancient Texts, The Book of Taliesin Peniarth MS 2,
    www.ancienttexts.org/library/celtic/ctexts/t13.html

National Library of Wales

www.britannica.com/topic/Mithraism

www.nessofbrodgar.co.uk/odinstone